I0473726

U.S. Department of Justice
Office of Justice Programs
810 Seventh Street N.W.
Washington, DC 20531

Janet Reno
Attorney General

Daniel Marcus
Acting Associate Attorney General

Mary Lou Leary
Acting Assistant Attorney General

Julie E. Samuels
Acting Director, National Institute of Justice

Office of Justice Programs	National Institute of Justice
World Wide Web Site	World Wide Web Site
http://www.ojp.usdoj.gov	*http://www.ojp.usdoj.gov/nij*

The Future of Forensic DNA Testing:

Predictions of the Research and Development Working Group

November 2000

NCJ 183697

Julie E. Samuels
Acting Director
National Institute of Justice

Christopher Asplen
Executive Director
National Commission on the Future of DNA Evidence

Opinions or points of view expressed are those of the authors and do not necessarily reflect the official position of the U.S. Department of Justice.

The National Institute of Justice is a component of the Office of Justice Programs, which also includes the Bureau of Justice Assistance, the Bureau of Justice Statistics, the Office of Juvenile Justice and Delinquency Prevention, and the Office for Victims of Crime.

Preface

The Research and Development Working Group was organized following a meeting of a planning panel on November 21, 1997. Starting early in 1998, the group has had several meetings and numerous exchanges by letter, e-mail, and telephone, and has arrived at a consensus regarding most of the items in this report. When there are differences, the alternatives are given. Likewise, we have tried to present the main alternative viewpoints of practitioners and observers in the field.

The report is divided into a summary and two main sections. The first of these, "Technology, Present and Future," is in nontechnical language and intended for a general readership. The second, "Appendix, Technical Summaries," is for those who want more details. These are followed by references, a list of abbreviations and acronymns, and a glossary.

Our specific assignment is to predict as well as we can where the technology will be in 5 years and in 10 years; we have included a 2-year projection. Our object has been to foresee what will happen, rather than to attempt to influence events. Therefore, the greatest use of our report should be for planning purposes. Nevertheless, several issues with legal and social implications arose in the meetings and were sometimes discussed. We do not take a position on these issues, but we do call them to the attention of others, including the National Commission on the Future of DNA Evidence.

One topic that might have been expected has not been discussed. This is the development and maintenance of laboratory standards. This area is the specific province of the DNA Advisory Board (DAB) and the Scientific Working Group on DNA Analysis Methods (SWGDAM), and for that reason we have stayed away from the subject.

We are greatly indebted to Lisa Forman for advice and for acting as liaison with the Commission. Robin Wilson has provided help in many ways, especially in organizing meetings and records. Finally, we thank Ranajit Chakraborty for unpublished data on population short tandem repeat (STR) frequencies throughout the world, John Buckleton for data on partial matches, Mark Batzer for information on Alu elements, John Butler for information on MALDI–TOF mass spectrometry, and Michael Hammer for data on Y chromosome DNA.

National Commission on the Future of DNA Evidence

The National Commission on the Future of DNA Evidence was created in 1998 at the request of Attorney General Janet Reno. When she read about the use of DNA to exonerate someone wrongfully convicted of rape and homicide, she became concerned that others might also have been wrongly convicted. The Attorney General then directed the National Institute of Justice (NIJ) to identify how often DNA had exonerated wrongfully convicted defendants. After extensive study, NIJ published the report *Convicted by Juries, Exonerated by Science: Case Studies in the Use of DNA Evidence to Establish Innocence After Trial,* which presents case studies of 28 inmates for whom DNA analysis was exculpatory.

On learning of the breadth and scope of the issues related to forensic DNA, the Attorney General asked NIJ to establish the Commission as a means to examine the future of DNA evidence and how the Justice Department could encourage its most effective use. The Commission was appointed by the former Director of the National Institute of Justice, Jeremy Travis, and represents the broad spectrum of the criminal justice system. Chaired by the Honorable Shirley S. Abrahamson, Chief Justice of the Wisconsin State Supreme Court, the Commission consists of representatives from the prosecution, the defense bar, law enforcement, the scientific community, the medical examiner community, academia, and victims' rights organizations.

The Commission's charge is to submit recommendations to the Attorney General that will help ensure more effective use of DNA as a crimefighting tool and foster its use throughout the entire criminal justice system. Other focal areas for the Commission's consideration include crime scene investigation and evidence collection, laboratory funding, legal issues, and research and development. The Commission's working groups, consisting of Commissioners and other non-Commission experts, research and examine various topics and report back to the Commission. The working group reports are submitted to the full Commission for approval, amendment, or further discussion and provide the Commission background for its recommendations to the Attorney General.

By nature of its representative composition and its use of numerous working groups, the Commission receives valuable input from all areas of the criminal justice system. The broad scope of that input enables the Commission to develop recommendations that both maximize the investigative value of the technology and address the issues raised by the application of a powerful technology.

Commission Members

Chair
The Honorable Shirley S.
    Abrahamson
Chief Justice
Wisconsin Supreme Court

Members
Dwight Adams
Section Chief
Scientific Analysis
Federal Bureau of
    Investigation

Jan S. Bashinski
Chief
Bureau of Forensic Services
California Department of
    Justice

George W. Clarke
Deputy District Attorney
San Diego, California

James F. Crow
Professor
Department of Genetics
University of Wisconsin

Lloyd N. Cutler
Wilmer, Cutler & Pickering
Washington, D.C.

Joseph H. Davis
Former Director
Miami-Dade Medical
    Examiner Department

Paul B. Ferrara
Director
Division of Forensic
    Sciences
Commonwealth of Virginia

Norman Gahn
Assistant District Attorney
Milwaukee County
Wisconsin

Terrance W. Gainer
Executive Assistant Chief
Metropolitan Police
    Department
Washington D.C.

Terry G. Hillard
Superintendent of Police
Chicago Police Department

Aaron D. Kennard
Sheriff
Salt Lake County, Utah

Philip Reilly
President and CEO
Shriver Center for Mental
    Retardation
Harvard University

Ronald S. Reinstein
Associate Presiding Judge
Superior Court of Arizona
Maricopa County

Darrell L. Sanders
Chief of Police
Frankfort, Illinois

Barry C. Scheck
Professor
Cardozo Law School
New York, New York

Kurt L. Schmoke
Mayor
Baltimore, Maryland

Michael Smith
Professor
University of Wisconsin
    Law School

Jeffrey E. Thoma
Public Defender
Mendocino County,
    California

Kathryn M. Turman
Director
Office for Victims of Crime
U.S. Department of Justice

William Webster
Milbank, Tweed, Hadley &
    McCloy
Washington, D.C.

James R. Wooley
Assistant U.S. Attorney
Cleveland, Ohio

Commission Staff
Christopher H. Asplen,
    AUSA
Executive Director

Lisa Forman, Ph.D.
Deputy Director

Robin S. Wilson
Executive Assistant

Research and Development Working Group Members

Chair
James F. Crow
Professor
Department of Genetics
University of Wisconsin

Members
Bruce Budowle
Program Manager, DNA Research
Forensic Science Research and Training Center
FBI Academy
Quantico, Virginia

Henry A. Erlich
Director, Department of Human Genetics
Roche Molecular Systems, Inc.
Alameda, California

Joshua Lederberg
Rockefeller University
New York, New York

Dennis J. Reeder
DNA Technologies Group
Biotechnology Division
National Institute of Standards and Technology
Gaithersburg, Maryland

James W. Schumm
Chief Scientist
The Bode Technology Group, Inc.
Springfield, Virginia

Elizabeth T. Thompson
Department of Statistics
University of Washington
Seattle, Washington

P. Sean Walsh
Genometrix
The Woodlands, Texas

Bruce S. Weir
William Neal Reynolds Professor of Statistics and Genetics
Department of Statistics
North Carolina State University
Raleigh, North Carolina

Contents

I. Summary

The principal assignment given to the Research and Development Working Group was to identify the technical advances in the forthcoming decade and to assess the expected impact of these on forensic DNA (deoxyribonucleic acid) analysis.

1. Past and Present Techniques

Progress in forensic analysis was slow until recently, but since 1985 more powerful techniques have increased explosively. The first useful marker system, the ABO blood groups, was discovered in 1900. The second, the MN groups, came a quarter century later. By the 1960s, there were 17 blood group systems known, but not all were useful for forensics, and in the 1970s a few serum proteins and enzymes were added. By the 1980s, some 100 protein polymorphisms were known but most were not generally useful for forensics.

The year 1985 brought a major breakthrough. VNTRs (variable number of tandem repeats) showed much greater variability among people than previous systems and immediately began to be used for forensic studies. They are still used, but are rapidly being replaced by STRs (short tandem repeats).

The great variability of DNA polymorphisms has made it possible to offer strong support for concluding that DNA from a suspect and from the crime scene are from the same person. Prior to this period, it was possible to exclude a suspect, but evidence for inclusion was weaker than it is now because the probability of a coincidental match was larger. DNA polymorphisms brought an enormous change. Evidence that two DNA samples are from the same person is still probabilistic rather than certain. But with today's battery of genetic markers, the likelihood that two matching profiles came from the same person approaches certainty.

Although the evidence that two samples came from the same person is statistical, the conclusion that they came from different persons is certain (assuming no human or technical errors). As a result of DNA testing, more than 70 persons previously convicted of capital crimes and frequently having served long prison terms have been exonerated. And there are everyday exculpations, since about a quarter of analyses lead to exclusions.

VNTRs are DNA regions in which a short sequence, usually 8 to 35 bases in length, is repeated in tandem 100 or more times. The exact number of repeats differs considerably from one person to another, so this provides an enormous amount of variability. The number of length-types that can be reliably distinguished is typically 20 to 30 per chromosomal locus. With 5 or 6 loci, the number of combinations is enormous and the probability of a random person's profile matching that of a suspect can be 1 in 100 billion or less.

STRs have a number of advantages compared to VNTRs. The most important is that, because of their smaller size, their DNA can be amplified by PCR (polymerase chain reaction). This is a procedure whereby a chosen region of DNA can be amplified by a process, much like that which occurs normally when DNA copies itself in a cell, which produces almost any desired amount. This means that DNA from a trace sample, such as that from a cigarette or the saliva on a postage stamp, can be increased to an amount that can be readily analyzed. The interpretation of STRs is usually less ambiguous than that of VNTRs and the process is more rapid—days instead of weeks. It also lends itself to automation, and kits are now available in which 16 loci can be analyzed simultaneously.

The Federal Bureau of Investigation (FBI) has chosen 13 STR loci to serve as core loci for the Combined DNA Index System (CODIS), the intention being that all forensic laboratories be equipped to handle these 13. Laboratories may, and usually do, have the capability of dealing with other loci as well.

In addition there are other systems. Single nucleotide polymorphisms (SNPs) detect changes in a single base of the DNA. There are millions of these per individual, so the opportunities for further exploitation are almost unlimited. They are widely used in the study of medical genetics and human evolution. A forensic example is HLA-DQA1. This has been used for some time and is still available. It is well known and quickly applied. It has been particularly useful for promptly clearing those suspects whose DNA does not match the evidence sample, thereby saving time and expense and avoiding unnecessary anguish. A wrongly accused innocent person has about a 95 percent chance of being cleared. Combining this with five other loci of the polymarker system, this probability is raised to 99.9 percent. SNPs usually have only two alleles.

Mitochondrial DNA (mtDNA) is found in the mitochondria, which are tiny organelles in the cell, not associated with the nuclear chromosomes. They are transmitted by the egg, but not by the sperm. Therefore, mtDNA is particularly useful in the study of people related through the female line. It is also particularly useful for another reason: Since there are numerous mitochondria per cell, a much smaller amount of DNA can be analyzed than if it were chromosomal DNA, for example, DNA in a shed hair. Alternatively, the Y chromosome is transmitted from father to all his sons, so DNA on the Y chromosome can be used to trace the male lineage. Y markers are particularly useful in resolving DNA from different males, as with sexual assault mixtures.

CODIS is a national database and searching mechanism, which now utilizes the 13 core STR loci. The purpose is to identify potential suspects. To do this, the FBI facilitates cooperation and comparison between laboratories. More than 100 laboratories have now installed the CODIS system. By the end of 2000, approximately 300,000 STR profiles from convicted felons will be on file. The database for STRs is much smaller, but is being rapidly expanded.

We now turn to projections for the decade ahead. We emphasize, however, that although improvements are sure to come, the current methods are reliable and valid.

2. Technology Projections for 2002

In this period the shift from VNTRs to the CODIS 13 core STR loci will continue. By 2002, many laboratories will have the capability of studying additional loci so that data for 20 or more loci will be available for purposes other than databasing. We expect increasing use of mtDNA for analysis of DNA that is degraded or present in very limited amounts, and for tracing relatives. Numerous Y chromosome markers, both SNPs and STRs, will be available. Additional markers will be found as an outcome of the Human Genome Project, which by this time will be near completion. The population databases for various population groups collated by the FBI are now available electronically, and more data should be readily available within the next 2 years.

We can also expect improvements in collection and purification techniques. Automation will make the process more efficient and rapid, and we expect interpretative software for analysis of complex problems, such as mixtures. There also is progress toward miniaturization, using a combination of chip technology and molecular genetics. Portable, hand-held systems are now working in laboratory experiments; how soon these will be available for routine use is not clear.

We also expect an increasing amount of re-examination of cases in which the conviction was based on evidence other than DNA.

3. Technology Projections for 2005

By 2005, the CODIS database should be well established, with more than 1 million convicted felon profiles on file (assuming current funding levels continue). Interstate comparisons will be commonplace and international comparisons increasingly feasible, since 8 of the 10 STRs in the British offender database are included in the 13 core STR loci. Greater automation and higher throughput approaches will help reduce the backlog.

Formats that can analyze multiple STR loci in miniaturized, mobile instruments are promised and should be available by this time. We also expect improved sampling and storage techniques. Research in the human genome and clinical research will produce many more markers, some of which will be used to supplement the existing procedures. We also expect integration of computers and internet with analytical techniques to permit direct transmission of test data between laboratories.

4. Technology Projections for 2010

Of course, the farther we peer into the future, the cloudier is our vision. Nevertheless, we expect that, although better procedures will undoubtedly have been developed, the 13 core STR loci will still be the standard currency. The reason is that changing systems is expensive and inefficient, and a system that is in place and working well is likely to be continued.

There may be some transition to new technologies, mainly to supplement the standard STRs. SNPs will be widely used in medical and agricultural research, so there will be many opportunities to carry these over for forensic purposes. We therefore envisage additions to the STR loci for some casework.

Within 10 years we expect portable, miniaturized instrumentation that will provide analysis at the crime scene with computer-linked remote analysis. This should permit rapid identification and, in particular, quick elimination of innocent suspects.

By this time there should be a number of markers available that identify physical traits of the individual contributing the DNA. It should be possible, using this information, to narrow the search for a suspect, with consequent increases in the accuracy and efficiency of operation.

5. Statistical and Population Issues

Over the past 10 years, data on allele frequencies for VNTR loci have accumulated in large numbers for population groups throughout the world and in the United States. There are far too many genotypes in the population for all genotypic frequencies to be included in the database. Hence it is necessary to record allele frequencies and arrive at profile frequencies by use of population genetics theory.

In a large, randomly mating population, the frequency of a profile is given by the product rule, which states that the frequency of a multilocus genotype is given by the product of the allele frequencies, with a factor of two for heterozygotes (Equations 1 in section II, 7, p. 22). Although not exact, this is often a satisfactory approximation (NRC 1992, NRC 1996, DAB 2000).

The conditional match probability is the probability, given the profile of the evidence sample, that a random individual from the population shares this profile. In simple cases (e.g., a single evidence sample and single suspect), this is simply the frequency of the profile in the population and in traditional forensic practice is called the match probability. A very small match probability is a strong argument that the same person contributed the two samples.

The likelihood ratio (LR) gives the ratio of the match probability if the suspect contributed the evidence to the match probability if another, unrelated person did. The likelihood ratio multiplied by the prior odds gives the posterior odds that the suspect contributed the evidence. Thus far, American and British courts have been reluctant to introduce prior probabilities. A few observers have advocated using a range of priors, such as is occasionally done in paternity testing, but this is not current courtroom practice.

Population structure can be taken into account by the use of a corrective factor, which we designate by θ. The θ-corrected conditional match probability is then given by Equations 2 in section II, 7, p. 24. NRC 1996 recommended that these corrected formulae be used when there is reason to believe that the evidence and suspect samples came from individuals in the same subpopulation. Others (e.g., Evett and Weir 1998) argue that the conditional probability always be used. Empirical estimates of θ in the major United States populations are usually considerably less than 0.01. For such small values, the difference between using Equations 1 and 2 is relatively small, but for larger values such as 0.03, which has been employed for Native American populations, the difference can be substantial. For numerical examples, see p. 63.

When there is uncertainty about the population substructure, as with isolated tribes or communities, or possible unsuspected relatives, the Sib Method can be used. The conditional match probability for a pair of sibs is determined mainly by simple Mendelian rules and is relatively unaffected by allele frequencies (which may differ among population subgroups) and unsuspected substructure, inbreeding, or presence of relatives. Since no other relatives are as close as sibs, the match probability for sibs provides a rough upper limit for the actual match probability.

The differences in STRs are mainly between individuals rather than between group averages. This means that the necessity for group classification could be avoided by using an overall U.S. database and an appropriately increased value of θ. This has been advocated by some to avoid invoking any group identification. A θ value of 0.03 would usually be appropriate.

The FBI has introduced a criterion for individualization. In effect it says that if the probability of a specific match is considerably less than the reciprocal of the United States population, it can be stated that the source has been identified. Strictly, such an analysis can yield only probabilities. Absolute certainty is outside the realm of scientific inquiry, no matter how small the probabilities. Nevertheless, a high degree of confidence in individualization can be attained. The legal system may adopt such a criterion, not as a scientific statement, but as a practical definition for forensic purposes.

6. Conclusions

a. Although this report looks to the future, we emphasize that current state-of-the-art DNA typing is such that the technology and statistical methods are accurate and reproducible. Nothing in our predictions should be interpreted as casting doubt on the reliability and validity of DNA typing as currently practiced. Our predictions are based on the assumption that science is always evolving and will seek future improvements and alternative methods that are even better.

b. STRs have proved to be very satisfactory for forensic use and are being rapidly adopted by forensic laboratories. The difficulty and expense of changing well-established and reliable procedures will inhibit changes to other systems. For this reason, we believe that STRs will be the predominant procedure during the next decade.

c. Methods of automation, increasing the speed and output and reliability of STR methods, will continue. In particular we expect that portable, miniature chips will make possible the analysis of DNA directly at the crime scene. This can be telemetered to databases, offering the possibility of immediate identification.

d. Other systems such as SNPs, Alu sequences, mitochondrial DNA, and Y chromosome DNA will continue to be developed, but for the next decade their use will be mainly as a supplement to STRs rather than as a replacement.

e. Techniques for handling minute amounts of DNA or DNA that is badly degraded will become much better. In particular, mitochondrial DNA will probably play an increasing role in such difficult cases.

f. Databases of DNA profiles of convicted felons will be extensive and coordinated throughout the States. International comparisons will be feasible and increasingly common. The rate at which this is implemented is heavily dependent on funding.

g. With the current 13 core STR loci, it is generally possible to distinguish among individuals, including relatives as close as siblings, with a high degree of reliability. There may be a convention adopted that will enable a sufficiently low match probability to be regarded as identification, but this is a legal and social, not scientific, definition.

h. In the future, it is likely that an increasing number of suspects will be identified by database searches. The statistical interpretation is difficult, particularly if future databases include representatives of the population at large rather than convicted felons. Two procedures for dealing with this future possibility are given in section II, 7e, p. 26.

II. Technology, Present and Future

1. Introduction

The principal assignment given to the Research and Development Working Group was to identify the most likely technical advances in the forthcoming decade and to assess the impact that these would have on forensic DNA analysis. We were asked to consider 5- and 10-year periods, to which we have added a 2-year forecast. Accordingly, we have taken as our future milestones the beginnings of the years 2002, 2005, and 2010.

Of course, forecasting is a highly uncertain venture. The polymerase chain reaction (PCR) was a total surprise 15 years ago. Technical developments such as DNA microchips and expression arrays would not have been predicted 10 years ago. In view of the near-certainty of surprises, what we are providing must be regarded as guesses; but they are guesses informed by familiarity with the techniques, their forensic applications, and the current rate of technological improvement. Our crystal ball is undoubtedly clouded, but we believe not broken.

Although this report looks to the future, we emphasize that current state-of-the-art DNA typing is such that the technology and statistical methods are accurate and reproducible. Nothing in our predictions should be interpreted as casting doubt on the reliability and validity of DNA typing as currently practiced. Our predictions are consistent with the viewpoint that science is always evolving and will seek future improvements and alternative methods that are even better.

DNA has had an intensity of scrutiny far greater than the other methods of criminal investigation, such as ballistics, handwriting, lie detection, eyewitnesses, even fingerprinting. It has passed the test. The scientific foundations of DNA are solid. Any weaknesses are not at the technical level, but are in possible human errors, breaks in the chain of evidence, and laboratory failures. It is possible that the careful scrutiny that DNA has had will lead to a closer look at other methods. Recently, the Clinton Administration announced an increased budget for a computer analysis and unified national database for shell casings and bullets. This might provide an example of the kind of closer scrutiny that we envision.

We are aware that the technological and population developments that are discussed in this report have ethical and social dimensions. Our assignment is technology predictions, so we have stayed away from ethical pronouncements, leaving these to other working groups, the Commission as a whole, and the larger society. We have, however, taken note of some circumstances resulting from technical advances in which such issues are likely to arise.

The National Research Council (NRC) has issued two reports on DNA technology as applied to forensics (NRC 1992, 1996). These reports and recommendations therein provide the background for much of current forensic practice. The DNA Advisory

Board (DAB) was authorized by the DNA Identification Act of 1994 and was established in March 1995. Its scope of activity is "to develop, and if appropriate, periodically revise recommended standards for quality assurance, including standards for testing the proficiency of forensic laboratories, and forensic analysts, in conducting analyses of DNA." DAB was authorized for 5 years, but this period was recently extended by the FBI Director to December 31, 2000. At that time this function of DAB is expected to be taken over by the Scientific Working Group on DNA Analysis Methods (SWGDAM). Because of the NRC reports, DAB, and SWGDAM, we have not included discussions of laboratory standards, quality assurance, accreditation, and proficiency tests in this report.

In 1995, DAB was authorized to extend its scope of activity to include "statistical and population genetics issues affecting the evaluation of the frequency of occurrence of DNA profiles calculated from pertinent population databases." A report was forwarded to the Director of the FBI in April 2000 (DAB 2000). Since part of our report deals with these issues, we shall frequently refer to this DAB report.

2. Biological Background

Here we provide a minimum biological and genetic background and vocabulary required for understanding this report. Many readers will find this section redundant and may choose to move to the next one. For fuller accounts, see NRC (1992, 1996). An easy to read, yet accurate introduction to human genetics is given in the textbook by Mange and Mange (1999). For more details, see Snustad and Simmons (2000), Berg and Singer (1992), Lewin (1990), Watson et al. (1987), and Twyman (1998).

Each human individual is made up of several hundred million million microscopic **cells** (plus considerable noncellular material such as bones and water). Cells come in a variety of shapes and sizes. Some are rounded, some flat, some angular, some irregular, and some (e.g., nerve cells) have long projections. A typical cell, such as a white blood cell, is about 1/2,000-inch in diameter. The part of greatest genetic interest, the inner part or **nucleus**, is usually roughly spherical. All the cells in the body are descended from a single fertilized egg, which by successive divisions has produced the vast number and various cell types that the human body comprises. The nucleus contains a number of wormlike or threadlike microscopic bodies, called **chromosomes**. Each species has a characteristic number of chromosomes—a typical human cell has 46.

The nucleus of a fertilized human egg starts out with 23 chromosomes from the mother's egg and a corresponding set of 23 from the father's sperm. A sperm or egg cell, containing a single set of chromosomes, is said to be **haploid**. A cell with two sets, a total of 23 pairs or 46 chromosomes, is **diploid**. The fertilized egg divides into two, these two into four, and so on throughout embryonic development, and for many kinds of cells, throughout life. The process of cell division (**mitosis**) distributes these chromosomes precisely. Before the cell divides, each chromosome has split longitudinally into two, and one goes to each daughter cell. Thus, after cell division, each of the daughter cells has identical chromosomes, the same as in the parent cell. This precise process assures that every cell in the body has an identical 46-chromosome makeup in its nucleus. Yet, as always in biology, there are exceptions. A red blood cell has no nucleus and therefore no chromosomes. Sometimes the chromosomes divide without a cell division, doubling the number. Liver cells, for example, are usually **polyploid**, that is, having four or more sets of chromosomes. The great bulk of cells, however, play by the rules; they are nucleated and have 46 chromosomes. Sometimes, two embryos will develop from the same fertilized egg, either because the two cells separate after the first division and each develops separately or, more often, by the multicellular embryo dividing into two parts at a later stage. This leads to **identical twins**. They necessarily have identical chromosomes and resemble each other closely; the differences they possess are due to environmental factors and the vagaries of development.

In the formation of a sperm or egg, the chromosome number is halved (fortunately, for otherwise each generation would have twice as many chromosomes as the preceding). By the precise process of **meiosis**, the chromosomes are allocated so that each **gamete** (sperm or egg) has one representative of each pair, for a total of 23. The members of different pairs behave independently in meiosis. If the chromosome from the number 1 pair in a sperm is maternal, that is, derived from the mother, the chromosome from the number 2 pair is equally likely to be either maternal or paternal, and so on. For convenience, the human chromosomes are identified by number, starting with the largest. Most chromosomes have a short and a long arm, designated by p and q respectively. Hence, 7p designates the short arm of the 7th largest chromosome.[1]

The two members of a chromosome pair, as seen in the microscope, are identical in shape and size. There is, however, an exception, the sex chromosomes. In the human cell, the **Y chromosome** is much smaller than the **X chromosome**. A body cell from a female has two X chromosomes; a cell from a male has an X and Y. Through the process of meiosis, an egg has a single X chromosome (in addition to 22 other chromosomes, called **autosomes**). A sperm has either an X or a Y. The chance event at fertilization, whether the successful sperm carries an X or Y chromosome, determines whether the developing embryo will be female or male. The X and Y chromosomes are not numbered, so the chromosomes of a gamete are numbered 1 through 22, plus X or Y.

In the past, the study of human chromosomes was very difficult. In fact, the actual number was thought to be 48 until better techniques, discovered in 1958, showed the number to be 46. At that time it was still difficult to identify individual chromosomes and great skill was required. Now there are specific stains for each chromosome, so anyone with normal color vision can identify them.

Outside the nucleus of the cell are a number of different structures. Of greatest forensic interest are the thousand or more **mitochondria** in each cell. These tiny organelles are responsible for producing much of the energy for the various activities that the body performs. For genetic analysis, the most important property of mitochondria is that they are transmitted only by the egg, not the sperm. Although the sperm contains a small number of mitochondria, these do not enter the egg and are not transmitted to the children. Thus, an embryo gets all its mitochondria from its mother. The mother got her mitochondria from *her* mother, and so on back through the female ancestral line.

---

1. Because of earlier uncertainties in size measurements, chromosomes 21 and 22 were reversed; 21 is actually smaller than 22. But since chromosome 21, when present an extra time, produces a well-known disorder, trisomy 21 or Down syndrome, it seemed wiser not to change its erroneously assigned number.

Each chromosome appears in the microscope as a three-dimensional object, a condensed sausage-shaped blob, at some stages of the cell division cycle, and a long, often invisible thread at others. The core of the chromosome is a very long, extremely thin thread of deoxyribonucleic acid; henceforth we shall use its more familiar nickname, **DNA**. The DNA molecule in a chromosome is surprisingly long. A single human chromosome, as seen with an ordinary microscope, is about 1/5,000-inch long. Yet the DNA molecule in this chromosome is an inch or more in length, compacted into the chromosome by successive coiling and supercoiling. The total DNA in a human cell, if the DNA molecules of each chromosome were lined up end to end, would be some 6 feet in length.

The DNA molecule is a double thread, coiled into a helix. The genetically important constituents of DNA are four **nucleotides** (or **bases**), abbreviated A, T, G, and C. The double thread consists of two phosphate-sugar strands bridged by many pairs of nucleotides, AT, TA, GC, or CG. A always pairs with T and G with C. The DNA molecule can be thought of as a twisted rope ladder with four kinds of stairsteps. Each chromosome has the base pairs in a specific order. The genetic difference between one gene and another, or one person and another, is not in the kinds of base pairs; always the same four are used. It is the sequence in which these occur that determines genetic individuality. With an enormous number of base pairs (stairsteps), the number of orders (permutations) is astronomical. No wonder we are all different; yet at the DNA level we are remarkably alike, as the next paragraph will explain.

The chromosomes of a sperm or egg contain about 3 billion base pairs, so a body cell has 6 billion. The whole set of base pairs in a gamete is the **genome**. The precise processes of DNA duplication and cell division ensure that each cell (with few exceptions, to be discussed later) contains the same sequence of DNA bases. Any two human genomes are alike for the overwhelming majority of their bases; DNA samples from two unrelated persons differ on the average at only about one base per thousand. Yet 1/1,000 of 6 billion is 6 million. These 6 million base differences are sufficient to produce all the genetic differences of those two persons. Although any two genomes differ at some 1/1,000 of their bases, these are not necessarily the same bases as those that are different in another pair of genomes. So the great diversity of shapes, sizes, color, behavior, disease susceptibility, and so on that characterize humanity is no surprise. Even though two persons share an overwhelming proportion of their DNA, there are still enough differences that no two are genetically alike, unless they are identical twins. If we had the complete sequence of the DNA from two persons, or even 1 percent of the DNA, we could (except for identical twins) be certain whether they came from one person or two. In practice, as will be discussed later, a much smaller fraction is analyzed, so that identification becomes probabilistic rather than certain.[2]

2. The great basic genetic similarity of all humans is one of the major lessons of molecular biology. Furthermore, the DNA of different species are often much alike; very similar genes occur in men, mice, and fruit flies, often with the same effect, although sometimes with quite different results. A typical human and chimpanzee differ at only about 1 percent of their DNA sites. Yet the two DNAs are readily distinguished, although a tiny fraction of DNA might not be. Of course we often pay more attention to the minority fractions of the genome that determine hair, speech, and brains, in which differences are more apparent than in the large unseen majority that we share.

In addition to differences in individual nucleotides, there are also variations in their number. There are some DNA regions in which a small number of bases is repeated a variable number of times, so the total amount of DNA in different individuals is not *exactly* the same. Some of the regions that are of the greatest use forensically are such repeated sequences in which the number of repeats varies from person to person.

At present, the Human Genome Project is nearing completion. In June 2000 it was about 90 percent complete. The object is to determine the complete sequence of base pairs in a representative person or a composite of several persons. Soon we shall know the complete encoded genetic information in a genome. This contains the totality of the genetic instructions in an egg or sperm, which together with all of the environmental influences determine the developmental outcome. The chromosomal DNA is not quite the totality of the biological inheritance, for a tiny fraction of the genetic information transmitted from one generation to the next is in the maternally transmitted mitochondria.

A **gene** is a stretch of DNA from 1,000 to 100,000 or more base pairs in length that has a specific function; usually a gene is responsible for a particular protein. Alternative forms of the gene are called **alleles**. For example, a specific allele of a particular gene is responsible for the enzyme that converts the amino acid phenylalanine into tyrosine. When this enzyme is missing or abnormal, the child develops the disease, phenylketonuria, or PKU. The result is severe mental retardation unless the child is treated; happily, with a specific diet the child develops normally. A child will develop PKU only if both representatives of the appropriate chromosome pair carry the abnormal allele. If there is only one PKU allele and the other is normal, the child will be normal; the amount of enzyme produced by a single normal allele is enough. Alleles that express their characteristic trait only when present in duplicate, like the PKU allele, are **recessive**. Those, like the normal allele, that are effective when present singly, are **dominant**. It is customary to designate genes by letter symbols, so we can designate the PKU allele by *a* and the normal alternative by *A*. An individual with two representatives of the same allele, *aa* or *AA*, is **homozygous** (noun: homozygote). If the two are different, *Aa*, the individual is **heterozygous** (noun: heterozygote). Finally, we need two more words. **Genotype** is the genetic makeup of the individual, such as *AA* or *Aa*. The genotypic designation may be extended to include several gene loci. **Phenotype** is the trait, such as mental retardation if observed externally or the metabolic defect if measured chemically. It may include several traits or it may be a quantitative measure such as height.

The rules of inheritance can be deduced from the behavior of chromosomes in meiosis and fertilization. However, before the mechanism of inheritance was understood, the rules were inferred by the Austrian monk, Gregor Mendel, from his experiments breeding garden peas. Although his studies were reported in 1865, they remained unknown until the principles were rediscovered in 1900. It was immediately obvious that Mendel's hereditary factors followed the same rules as chromosomes; hence the genes must be carried by chromosomes.

As stated earlier, the human chromosomes are numbered from 1 to 22, starting with the largest, plus the X and Y. Each gene occupies a specific position (or **locus**) on a specific chromosome. The gene causing PKU is at a locus on 12q, meaning that it is on the long arm of chromosome number 12. Typically, there are more than two different alleles at a locus in a population. There may be hundreds in some extreme cases, but of course any fertilized egg has at most two kinds. A locus with more than one allele in the population is said to be **polymorphic**. Highly polymorphic loci are particularly useful for forensic identification.[3]

In the process of meiosis, one member of each chromosome pair is included in the gamete. Early in meiosis, the two homologous chromosomes pair up. While lined up side by side they often break at corresponding sites and exchange partners. Thus, two genes that were formerly on the same chromosome may end up on different chromosomes, if there has been an exchange between them. The tendency for two different genes on the same chromosome to be inherited together is called **linkage**. The closer together two genes are on the chromosome, the less probable it is that a break will occur between them and the more probable that they are to be inherited together. This property has been used in classical genetics to "map" the position of genes on the chromosome; the closer together two genes are, the more tightly linked they are in inheritance. This method, developed in experimental animals, also is used to locate genes on human chromosomes, although in recent times it is often supplemented by more direct physical means.[4]

Genes are ordinarily transmitted from generation to generation unchanged. Sometimes, however, the gene is changed, a rare process called **mutation**. For example, the normal allele may change to the one causing PKU. When a gene mutates, the mutant form is as stable and as regularly transmitted as the original. Mutations come in all sizes. A mutation may be a substitution of one base for another, or one or more bases may be gained or lost, or the order of a group of bases may be changed, inverted for example. Chromosomes are sometimes broken and reattached in new ways. Or a whole chromosome may be lost or duplicated. All of these come under the general name of mutation, although the term is more often restricted to those changes that are transmitted as a Mendelian unit.

The genes make up only a tiny fraction of the DNA. The rest, the great bulk—about 97 percent—has no known function. It is sometimes referred to as "junk DNA." Nevertheless, these nongenic regions show the same genetic variability that genes do, in fact usually more. These differences are not overt, but can be detected by laboratory tests. Regions of DNA that are used for forensic analysis are usually not genes, but rather are located in those parts of the chromosomes without known functions, or if part of a gene, not in the part that produces a detectable effect. (One reason for this choice has been to protect individual privacy.) Nevertheless, the words commonly used for describing genes (e.g., allele, homozygous, polymorphic) are carried over to DNA regions used for identification. It is customary to call the genotype for the group of loci involved in a forensic analysis a **profile**.

---

3. Very rare alleles are not considered in designating a locus as polymorphic. A common definition says that the locus is polymorphic if the most common allele has a frequency of less than 99 percent.

4. Human genetic study and chromosome mapping in particular are much more complicated than in experimental organisms, where specific matings producing large numbers of progeny can determine gene order simply and accurately. Human pedigrees are complicated and of course not arranged for the convenience of curious geneticists. Thus, complicated statistics and computer routines are required to elicit information that would often be trivially simple in experimental organisms. Despite this limitation, thanks to a very large number of molecular markers discovered in recent years, the human gene map is as detailed as that of any experimental species. Tens of thousands of loci have been mapped.

In DNA, the chemical bonds that hold the two parts of a stairstep—AT, TA, CG, or GC—are weaker than those that hold the steps to the coiled upright. Therefore, the DNA ladder tends to fall apart into two single uprights with half steps protruding. Such single-stranded DNA is said to be **denatured**. Denaturing can be produced by a simple temperature rise, or it can be induced by chemicals. A single strand of DNA has a tendency to pair up with a complementary single strand, that is with one that has an A every time the original strand has a T, and so on. It is this process of highly specific pairing of single-stranded, complementary DNAs that is the basis for forensic use of DNA. A DNA **probe** is a short segment of single-stranded DNA, usually labeled by being attached to a radioactive atom or a chemical dye, which is complementary to a designated chromosomal region. Finally, there are enzymes (**restriction enzymes**) that seek out a specific region of the DNA and cut it. For example, the enzyme HaeIII finds the sequence GGCC, or CCGG on the other strand, and cuts both DNA strands between G and C. (More properly, the other strand is written in reverse order, because of the opposite polarity of the two DNA strands.) Among the 3 billion base pairs in the genome, there are millions of GGCC sequences. So treatment with HaeIII cuts the DNA into millions of pieces, the size of each piece depending on how far apart the adjacent GGCC sequences happen to be.

The loci that have been most extensively used for forensics are regions in which a short segment of DNA is repeated tandemly many times. For example, a length of 20 bases may be repeated dozens or even hundreds of times. Such long sequences are much more mutable than genes usually are, the mutations being an increase or decrease in length. If the DNA is cut by a restriction enzyme on both sides of such a region, the region may be isolated and its size measured. Thus, different numbers of repeats are identified by their size. A polymorphism that is recognized by different sizes of such fragments is called a restriction fragment length polymorphism, or **RFLP**.

The way in which these properties are put to use in DNA identification will be discussed later.

3. History, Before 1985

The first genetic markers that were useful for human identification were the ABO blood groups discovered in the same year (1900) that Mendel's rules of inheritance were rediscovered. Nineteenth century scientists, investigating the causes of blood-transfusion reactions, mixed the bloods from different individuals in the laboratory. They soon discovered that when the bloods were incompatible, a clumping or precipitation of the red blood cells occurred. This allowed the scientists to identify the cell surface elements (called **antigens**) responsible for the reaction. They noted that human blood cells fell in four antigenic groups which Landsteiner (1900) designated A, B, AB, and O. It was quickly realized that the blood groups were inherited, but despite the seeming simplicity of the system, the genetic basis remained unclear. It was not until 1925 that the mode of inheritance was inferred from the population frequencies of the four groups (using gene-frequency methods that will be employed later in this report).

Different human populations were found to differ in the frequencies of the four types. For example, about 10 percent of Caucasian Americans are group B. If one of two blood samples was group A and the other group B, they must have come from different persons (in the absence of laboratory or other errors). On the other hand, if both were group

B they could have come from the same person, but they could also have come from two different persons, each of whom happened to be group B. Over the years, several more independently inherited red blood cell systems were discovered. By 1960 there were some 17 systems, but not all were useful for identification. The most useful was the so-called HLA system because it was highly polymorphic (i.e., with many alleles). Along with this battery of serological tests some laboratories included a few serum proteins and enzymes. Although it was quite probable that two blood samples from different persons would agree for one blood group or enzyme, it was less and less probable that two unrelated persons would agree for all loci as more tests were added.

The frequencies of a combination of such markers were typically one in a few hundred or less, although in some instances, when samples contained rare types, the probability of matching of samples could be much smaller. By the mid-1970s, analysis of evidence samples and calculations of random matches could be calculated. A combination of blood groups and serum proteins were sometimes used for identification in criminal investigations. Much more often, such probabilities were used in paternity testing and accepted as evidence of parentage, where the civil criterion "preponderance of evidence," rather than the criminal criterion "beyond reasonable doubt," prevailed.

For parentage analysis, a **paternity index** is calculated. This is the probability of the mother-child-man combination if the man is the father divided by the probability if the father were randomly chosen from the population. There are differences from State to State as to the value of the paternity index that is regarded as sufficient evidence. A value of 100 is common, but smaller values prevail in some States. For a full discussion, see Walker (1983).[5]

Criminal cases require a higher standard of proof. Although a combination of blood groups and serum proteins often gave very small probabilities for a match between two unrelated individuals, and were sometimes used in criminal investigations, more powerful methods were desirable. These came with the discovery of a different kind of polymorphism, to which we now turn.

4. The VNTR (RFLP) Period, 1985–1995

The nature of forensic identification changed abruptly in 1985. That year Alec Jeffreys and colleagues in England first demonstrated the use of DNA in a criminal investigation (Jeffreys et al. 1985a,b). He made use of DNA regions in which short segments are repeated a number of times. This number of repeats varies greatly from person to person (Wyman and White 1980). Jeffreys used such variable-length segments of DNA, first to exonerate one suspect in two rape homicides of young girls and later to show that another man had a DNA profile matching that of the sperm in the evidence samples from

---

5. A paternity index of 100 is sometimes called the "odds of paternity." But this is not the true odds of paternity; rather, it is the ratio of the probability of the mother-child-man combination if the man is the father to the probability if a random man is the father. The human psyche seems to have an overwhelming proclivity to misinterpret this. For a typical example, a recent newspaper story said: "Judge ____ released the results of DNA tests that showed that there is a 99.9 percent probability that ____ is the father of ____."

both girls. Soon after, some commercial laboratories made use of this "fingerprinting" procedure,[6] and in 1988 the FBI implemented the techniques, after improving their robustness and sensitivity and collecting extensive data on the frequency of different repeat lengths in different populations.

The DNA methods offered a number of advantages compared to the earlier systems. One advantage is that these tests are based directly on the genetic makeup of the individual, the DNA itself. In contrast, serological and protein tests identify a gene product and therefore may be only an indirect reflection of the DNA composition. DNA methods avoid any complication from dominance and recessiveness. For example, with dominance, genotypes *AA* and *Aa* are indistinguishable phenotypically, but can be distinguished by DNA methods. Furthermore, DNA markers offer greater stability against temporal and thermal changes than proteins. In fact, DNA is remarkably stable, as is evidenced by its being identified long after death, for example, in Egyptian mummies or even extinct mammoths. Since DNA is found in cells throughout the body, the material to be tested can come from any source of cells. A blood or semen stain, even one that is several years old, can often be analyzed. Most important, from a forensic standpoint, individual variability in the DNA is much greater than can be revealed by serological and enzymatic markers, so that the probability of two unrelated individuals having the same DNA profile is very small. The large number of alleles per locus and the number of loci that can be used as genetic markers permitted forensic scientists to have access to a large panel of stable genetic markers for the first time. Thus, DNA held the potential, when a sufficient number of sufficiently variable markers were identified, to supply strong support for identity between, for example, a crime scene sample and DNA from a suspect.

After a first flush of immediate acceptance by the courts, the molecular methodology and the results of evidence analysis were challenged as unreliable. Although the majority of courts admitted the DNA evidence, a few highly publicized cases were overturned by higher courts, citing failure of sufficient DNA testing to meet the Frye or other standards for admissibility of scientific evidence as the reason. During this period, partly because of these challenges, the technical standards for forensic DNA testing improved greatly and the databases used to generate statistical frequencies became more extensive and more representative. As the forensic DNA community imposed stringent quality control and quality assurance protocols on their laboratories and published numerous validation studies, the DNA profiling techniques became widely accepted by the courts and relied upon by juries. By 1996, a study by the National Research Council (NRC 1996) concluded that: "The state of profiling technology and the methods for estimating frequencies and related statistics have progressed to the point where the admissibility of properly collected and analyzed data should not be in doubt."

VNTRs (variable number of tandem repeats), a type of RFLP, are based on the methods Jeffreys used. These are DNA sequences of a length from 8 to 80 base pairs (usually 15 to 35) that are repeated in tandem different numbers of times in different alleles. At a particular locus, the number of repeats can be several hundred and the total size of the sequence can be 10,000 base pairs or more. The VNTR procedure is described and discussed more fully in appendix A1.a. In practice the size differences among repeated

---

6. In this report, we shall not use the words fingerprint or fingerprinting in order not to confuse DNA testing with dermal fingerprints. We shall ordinarily use "profiling" for the process of determining the relevant DNA genotype.

sequences are so small that adjacent sizes cannot be reliably distinguished, so they are grouped into 20 or 30 "bins." With this many alternatives (alleles), the probability of two random DNA samples having the same pattern at a single locus is small, and when data are combined over four to six independently inherited loci the probabilities become very small. With 6 loci the probability of 2 random Caucasian Americans sharing the same profile is less than 1 in 100 billion (appendix A1.a, p. 38). This calculation, using the "product rule" assumes that the genotypes are in random proportions within and between loci. (For a discussion of the accuracy of this assumption, see NRC 1996, pp. 89–112).[7]

Although there is more variability within groups than between the means of different groups, allele frequencies between groups differ enough that separate databases have been developed for Caucasian Americans, African Americans, Hispanic Americans, and Asian Americans. Increasingly, there are data on smaller subpopulations, such as American Indian tribes.[8]

VNTRs have both advantages and limitations. The main advantages are: (1) The large number of alleles per locus and combining several loci provide a very high discriminating power; (2) the large number of alleles make this approach particularly effective in resolving mixtures of DNA from different persons; and (3) large databases from several population groups are available as a basis for calculations.

Yet there are several limitations to VNTRs: (1) The small differences between adjacent alleles necessitates grouping them into bins, which complicates the statistical analysis; (2) the number of validated loci is limited; (3) relatively large amounts of high-quality DNA are required; (4) a single band is sometimes ambiguous, for it may be from a homozygote or it may be from a heterozygote in which (for a variety of reasons) only one band appears; and (5) the process is time consuming, particularly if radioactive probes are used. An analysis of multiple loci can require several weeks. However, radioactive probes have largely been replaced by chemiluminescent probes and the process now takes only days rather than weeks.

VNTRs are being rapidly replaced by repeats of shorter sequences, to which we now turn.

---

7. In forensic cases, investigators usually know the profile of the evidence sample and ask for the probability that DNA from a random person matches this profile. This is called the match probability, or more precisely the conditional match probability. For evaluating the power of different systems used in forensic analyses it is customary to use the probability of a random pair of persons sharing a profile. That is the sum of the match probabilities for all possible pairs. We shall refer to this as the population match probability.

8. There is a great deal of confusion, controversy, and political sensitivity about the use of words like "race," "ethnic group," "geographical group," and "biological ancestry." Such classifications are often ambiguous; in fact, the classification is sometimes linguistic or geographical rather than biological, as with Hispanic Americans. We have chosen to use **population group** for larger groups such as Caucasian Americans and African Americans and **subgroup** for smaller groups such as northern and southern Europeans. Throughout this report, we emphasize that with the increasing power of DNA profiling we can move away from emphasis on group properties to emphasis on individual properties.

5. Current Techniques

During the decade 1985–1995, a revolutionary technical innovation became more and more widely used in molecular biology, so that by now it is almost universal. This is the polymerase chain reaction (PCR), a technique for amplifying a tiny quantity of DNA into almost any desired amount (Saiki et al. 1985, 1988; Mullis and Faloona 1987). It uses essentially the same principle as that by which DNA is normally copied in the cell, except that instead of a whole chromosome being copied only a short chosen segment of the DNA in a chromosome is amplified. This has made it possible to process the very tiny amounts of DNA often left behind as evidence of a crime and has greatly increased the sensitivity of the forensic systems available to the criminal justice system. Thanks to PCR, minute amounts of DNA extracted from hairs, postage stamps, cigarette butts, coffee cups, and similar evidence sources can often be successfully analyzed.

The first use of PCR-based typing for forensic application was in 1986 and employed the HLA-DQA1 locus (originally called DQ-α). Currently, this system distinguishes seven allelic classes, recognized by sequence-specific probes using a technique called reverse dot blot (appendix A2.b, p. 44). In this method, amplified DNA is captured from solution by probes that are fixed to a membrane. The hybridized DNAs are detected with a nonradioactive blue stain. With this system, the general probability of matching profiles, for example between a forensic sample from the crime scene and a random suspect, is about 0.05. Thus, 95 percent of wrongly accused persons can expect to be cleared. This makes the system particularly useful for early testing in criminal investigation with a large probability of quickly clearing wrongly identified suspects.

In addition to the HLA-DQA1 locus, five additional genetic markers became available to the forensic community in 1993, adding increased discriminatory power to the reverse dot blots for forensic case work (see appendix A2.c, p. 44). The six-locus system (the poly-marker system + DQA) has been in wide use in public and private forensic laboratories and the results are widely accepted in U. S. courts. The five additional markers are 2- and 3-allele loci, so, while they increase the discriminatory power of HLA-DQA1 alone, the set still falls short of VNTRs in this respect. The probability of a match for two randomly chosen persons is about 1/4,000 (see table A3, p. 45).

The D1S80 locus is a 16 base-pair repeat VNTR that is small enough to be amplified by PCR. It is amplified as a "singleplex," run on vertical acrylamide gels and detected by silver staining, or as a duplex with the sex-determining amelogenin (see below). Allele designations are accomplished by comparison with allelic ladders that are run on adjacent lanes in the gel. This bridges the gap between VNTR and STRs in the development of systems based on length polymorphism. D1S80 is fully validated and accepted by the courts. It is commonly used in combination with the reverse dot blot tests to extend their statistical power. It is used in casework, but is not for databases.

STRs (short tandem repeats) (see appendix A1.b, p. 39) are similar to VNTRs in that they are based on repeated sequences dispersed throughout the chromosomes. While methods of interpretation for STRs and VNTRs are similar, STRs have smaller repeat units (usually 3 to 5 base pairs) and fewer of them (usually 7 to 15 alleles per locus). The small size makes them amenable to PCR amplification so that much smaller quantities of DNA are needed for analysis.[9] The small size also allows improved visualization of each allele so discrete and unambiguous allele determinations are possible and grouping multiple adjacent alleles into bins is not needed. Although VNTRs include more alleles per locus, STR loci are much more numerous, providing the same discriminating power by using more loci. In addition, multiple STR loci can be analyzed simultaneously (**multiplexed**), a practice uncommon in VNTR analysis. Multiplexing of STR systems has become standard, increasing the efficiency, speed, and power of analysis. With 13 STR loci the general match probability is about one in 6×10^{14} (A1.b, table A2, p. 41).

Having more loci, once there are several alleles per locus, is particularly important if siblings are involved. The match probability between two siblings always involves a factor of 1/4 per locus, plus an additional, usually smaller quantity that depends on allele frequencies. Thus, adding more alleles per existing locus when the heterozygosity is already large is of only marginal help in increasing the ability to discriminate between siblings; adding additional loci is much more effective, but these should be highly polymorphic.

It is often important, especially in rape cases, to determine the sex of the person from which the DNA came. If the source is vaginal, it is important to distinguish between female cells and sperm. For this, a marker that is on the X and Y chromosomes is used. Amelogenin is a PCR-amplified system that can be combined with STRs. The allele on the X has a different size than the one on the Y, so the difference between XY males and XX females is easily seen.

Techniques for using mitochondrial DNA (mtDNA) (see appendix A3.a, p. 46) have been available for some years, but application to problems of forensic identification began in 1990. Several laboratories now have the necessary equipment and techniques to use this system. Mitochondria are intracellular particles (organelles) outside the nucleus in the cytoplasm of the cell. They contain their own small DNA genomes; circular molecules of 16,569 base pairs and the variants are identified by sequence determination. Each cell contains hundreds to thousands of mitochondria. For this reason, a single hair shaft, old bones, or charred remains, which are generally unsuitable for chromosomal DNA, sometimes provide enough intact material for mtDNA analysis. Mitochondria are transmitted by the egg but not by the sperm, so mtDNA is uniquely suited for tracing ancestry through the female line. It was used recently to identify some of the bodies of the Russian royal family, the Romanovs. Limitations of mtDNA include its relatively low discriminatory power and the dependence for that power on the creation of large databases of mtDNA sequences.

Sperm cells contain mitochondria, although in much smaller numbers than in body cells (about 50 compared to 1,000 or more). This part of the sperm does not enter the egg, so only the maternal mitochondria are normally transmitted to the children. It is possible by existing techniques to analyze mtDNA from sperm. This has been done in laboratory experiments, but has not been developed for routine use in forensics. This might be useful in cases where a tiny amount of semen is available and no other source of DNA.

---

9. The PCR process can be used only on relatively short DNA segments. Almost all VNTRs are too large, and this is one of the reasons why VNTRs are being replaced by STRs. Recently, a technique for amplifying longer fragments has been reported (Richie et al. 1999). Since STRs are rapidly becoming the standard, this new technique will probably be used only for cases where there is a need for additional, highly polymorphic loci.

This will become especially useful when it is possible to amplify and analyze mtDNA from a single sperm. Some research laboratories have already done this. For nuclear DNA, a single sperm provides only a 50-percent sample of the individual's DNA, so that several sperm cells are required for complete information. Each mitochondrion, in contrast, has the entire mitochondrial genome.

The Y chromosome (see appendix A3.b, p. 49) contains hundreds of recognized sites that can be used for identification. These consist of both STRs and single nucleotide polymorphisms (SNPs). The Y chromosome provides a counterpart to mtDNA. Since the Y chromosome is transmitted only from father to son, it provides a way of tracing male descent much as mtDNA does for the female lineage. They differ, however, in that mtDNA is a cytoplasmic marker transmitted in multiple copies from the mother to *all* her children, whereas Y chromosome DNA is a nuclear marker transmitted as a single copy from the father to sons only. Y chromosome markers can be useful in special cases resolving sexual assault mixtures from multiple male contributors, when the male component of the DNA is very small in proportion to the female component, or to distinguish mixtures of different male sources of saliva or blood. Such sex-specific markers are finding a major use outside the criminal field, as exemplified by the recent study of Thomas Jefferson's male descendants. As with mtDNA, the loci on the relevant part of the Y chromosome almost never recombine, so the Y chromosome markers are equivalent to one locus with many alleles. Therefore, the discriminating power is limited by the size of the database. Y chromosome markers reveal more diversity than other markers with respect to ancestral geographic origin, and for this reason they find special application in studies of human evolution.

6. CODIS (Combined DNA Index System)

The FBI has selected 13 STR loci to serve as a standard battery of **core** loci, and increasingly laboratories are developing the capability to process these loci. As laboratories throughout the Nation employ the same loci, comparisons and cooperation between laboratories are facilitated. The 13 loci and some of their properties are given in appendix A1.b, p. 41. Collectively, the 13 loci provide great discriminatory power. The probability of a match between profiles of two unrelated persons in a randomly mating population of Caucasian Americans is 1.74×10^{-15}, or one in 575 trillion. The FBI and others are actively involved in getting frequency data from a number of populations of different population groups and subgroups. These populations are being continuously subdivided. For example, there are data from Japanese, Chinese, Korean, and Vietnamese. In the Western Hemisphere, there are data for Bahamians, Jamaicans, and Trinidadians. With the 13 core loci the most common profile has an estimated frequency less than 1 in 10 billion (Budowle et al. 1999). Of the 10 STR loci that the British system now uses, 8 are included in the 13 core loci, so international comparisons are feasible.

The FBI provides software to facilitate the use of the CODIS system, together with installation, training, and user support free of charge to any State and local law enforcement laboratories providing DNA analysis. CODIS uses two indices to generate investigative leads in crimes where there is DNA evidence. The Convicted Offender Index contains profiles of individuals convicted of violent crimes. The Forensic Index contains DNA profiles from crime scene evidence, such as semen and blood. These indices are searched by computer.

The CODIS system stores the information necessary for determining a match (a specimen identifier, the sponsoring laboratory's identifier, the names of laboratory personnel who produced the profile, and the DNA profile). To ensure privacy, it does not include such things as social security numbers, criminal history, or case-related information.

By the year 2000, more than 100 laboratories had installed CODIS. Searches may be conducted at three tiers: local, State, and national. The CODIS database from convicted felons in July 1998 had more than 230,000 VNTR profiles. Approximately 300,000 samples will be analyzed for STRs by the end of 2000, but the backlog of unanalyzed convicted offender samples is still more than 600,000 (FBI 1999). We anticipate that substantial reduction of the backlog will require 2 to 5 years, depending strongly on funding.

The selection of the 13 core STR loci will stimulate additional growth of databases using these loci. This investment in the database makes it likely that the core loci will be employed, with possible additions, throughout the periods covered by this report.

7. Statistical and Population Considerations

a. Statistical Procedures

A typical situation is this: A DNA sample is obtained from the crime scene and DNA from a suspect is found to have the same profile. This may be because the crime-scene DNA came from the suspect. It may also be because the perpetrator and the suspect happen to have the same profile. There are several approaches to deciding between these possibilities (NRC 1996, DAB 2000).

The mere fact that the two DNA samples have matching profiles is a general statement providing evidence of a sort. But to convey the weight of evidence this needs the support of a probabilistic analysis.

The traditional procedure; profile probability. The profile probability is the probability that a person chosen at random from the relevant population has the DNA profile of the reference sample (e.g., that of the crime scene sample). The probability of this profile is estimated from the allelic frequencies in the database, as described in the next section. The rarer the profile, the stronger is the evidence that the two DNA samples came from the same person.

Consider a typical case. The profile is determined from the evidence taken from the crime scene. Before the suspect is identified, the probability of this profile in a person randomly chosen from the relevant population is P. A suspect is found and his DNA matches that of the evidence. Then, if P is a very small fraction, we can say that either the two DNA samples came from the same person or a very improbable event has occurred, namely, that two different persons happened to have the same profile.

This approach has been used repeatedly for criminal cases since the earliest days of DNA evidence (see NRC 1992, NRC 1996, DAB 2000), and earlier for civil cases when other kinds of markers were used (Walker 1983). It is widely accepted and is the most commonly used procedure in U. S. courts and in the scientific community. We shall refer to it as the "traditional" method. Its simplicity is appealing to many analysts.

Likelihood ratio. Alternatively, we can use the likelihood ratio (LR) approach, which has long been employed in paternity testing and human genetics. In this approach, we compute the probability of the DNA evidence under two hypotheses. In the simple case where the evidence is the profiles of the crime sample and a suspect, the two hypotheses might be H1: the two profiles are from the same person, and H2: the two profiles are from different, unrelated persons. The likelihood ratio is the ratio of the probability of the evidence under H1 divided by the probability of the evidence under H2. In symbols, letting E stand for the evidence (i.e., the two profiles), $LR = Pr(E|H1)/Pr(E|H2)$. The joint probabilities of the two profiles can be rewritten as conditional probabilities of either profile, given the other one. This leads to, for example, LR = Pr(suspect profile|crime sample profile and H1)/Pr (suspect profile|crime sample profile and H2). Under hypothesis 1, the probability is one, since the two profiles must be the same if they came from the same person (assuming no errors). The denominator is the probability of a person chosen randomly from the population having the matching profile, given that the crime sample has the profile. A LR of 100 means that the evidence is 100 times as probable if the suspect is the perpetrator (i.e., the source of the crime sample) as if the suspect was unrelated to the perpetrator.

In the simple case, the likelihood ratio is simply the reciprocal of the match probability. If knowledge of the crime sample profile does not affect the probability of a random person having the profile, the match probability is the same as the profile probability as employed in the traditional approach. Then there is little reason to prefer one procedure over the other, and courts have usually heard the profile probability. There are, however, reasons for using the likelihood ratio. One is that LR has useful statistical properties (see Royall 1997). A second is that in complicated cases, such as mixed samples, the LR provides a more direct and consistent approach (NRC 1996, pp. 129–130, 162–163; Evett and Weir 1998, pp. 188–205). A third reason is that the LR can be converted into a probability by using Bayes' Theorem, as we now explain.

Using Bayes' Theorem. Suppose that, in the absence of DNA evidence, there are certain odds (which we may or may not know) that the same person is the source of both DNA samples.[10] Then the effect of taking the DNA evidence into account is to multiply these odds by the likelihood ratio. It is customary to use the words "prior odds" for the odds not taking DNA into account and "posterior odds" when it is taken into account. Thus,

Posterior odds = Prior odds x LR.

The main problem with this Bayesian argument has been the uncertainty and subjective nature of the prior odds. They depend on the confidence one has in the other sources of information (e.g., detective work or the reliability of an eyewitness). It is difficult to assign a number to the prior odds. American and British courts have been reluctant to employ prior odds and Bayesian methods.[11]

---

10. **Odds and probability**. Suppose that P(A) is the probability of event A. The odds of A, O(A), are P(A)/[1 - P(A)] and P(A) = O(A)/[1 + O(A)].

11. In paternity testing it is often assumed, implicitly or explicitly, that the prior odds are 1:1. In that case the likelihood ratio (the Paternity Index) is the same as the posterior odds.

One approach that has sometimes been suggested is to present the court with a series of prior odds. Consider three prior odds in favor of the two samples coming from the same person: 100, 1, and 1/100. Suppose LR = 100 million. Then the posterior odds are 10 billion, 100 million, and 1 million, respectively. In this case, the DNA evidence is strong enough to overwhelm prior odds even though they differ by a factor of 10,000. With multiple loci, this will often be the case. Despite this procedure's being advocated by a few, it has not found acceptance by the courts.

Much of the published literature dealing with forensic evidence in recent years has centered on the use of likelihood ratios. See, for example, Aitken (1995), Balding and Donnelly (1995), Evett and Weir (1998), Robertson and Vigneaux (1992), and Royall (1997). Practicing criminalists, if they provide quantitative information, usually give just the profile probability. For most cases where there are only weak dependencies between suspect and crime sample profiles, this is appropriate. However, profile probabilities by themselves do not allow for a complete interpretation in cases of relatives, population structure, mixed stains, or database searches. In most cases likelihood ratios are the reciprocals of match probabilities, which are often larger than profile probabilities.

Some prefer the traditional procedure for simplicity. Simplicity is often acceptable and may be preferred as being more easily understood and acceptable by the courts. The traditional procedure has been endorsed by Chakraborty and Carmody (see Budowle, Chakraborty et al. 2000) and by the DNA Advisory Board (DAB 2000).

In its recent report, the DNA Advisory Board (DAB 2000) said: "As emphasized in the NRC II report, there are alternative methods for assessing the probative value of DNA evidence. Rarely is there only one statistical approach to interpret and explain the evidence." We emphasize that the two approaches discussed here essentially always lead to the same conclusion. A 13-locus STR match between unrelated individuals is a very rare event. The expected frequency of the most common 13-locus profile, using the product rule, is less than 1/10 billion in all populations studied (Budowle et al. 1999, p. 1284). A match strongly supports the conclusion that the two DNA profiles came from the same individual. The differing approaches should not throw doubt on the discriminating power of multilocus DNA profiles or imply that they are likely to lead to different conclusions.

b. Population Genetics

Within the last few years, the databases for STRs have become much more extensive. The sample sizes are larger and the population groups are more refined. In early analyses, the populations were assumed to be in random proportions within each locus, known as the Hardy-Weinberg rule. It was also assumed that the population was at equilibrium between loci, called linkage equilibrium. These two assumptions form the basis for the traditional procedures for calculating match probabilities.

Single locus; the Hardy-Weinberg rule. Letting A_i and A_j designate alleles and p_i and p_j their frequencies in the population, then the HW rule predicts that the genotype proportions are

Homozygotes: $P(A_iA_i) = p_i^2$. (1a)

Heterozygotes: $P(A_iA_j) = 2p_ip_j$. (1b)

The assumption underlying this rule is that the population is mating at random with respect to this locus, that is, mates are chosen without regard to these genotypes. The HW proportions are attained in a single generation. This simple principle is not exact, of course, but it is frequently a satisfactory approximation to a real human population.

Earlier reports (e.g., NRC 1996) concluded that departures from Hardy-Weinberg ratios for VNTRs are quite minor. Recent studies of STRs show similar results. For example, an exact test for departures from HW proportions at 13 STR loci in three populations—Caucasian American, African American, and Hispanic American—showed only very minor departures from expectations, and none were statistically significant. These were mainly genotypes with very rare alleles, where chance deviations are expected. In fact the whole distribution agreed very well with HW expectations (Lins et al. 1998; Budowle et al. 1999).

Multiple loci: Linkage equilibrium (LE). With random mating the relationship between loci approaches random proportions. That is, the frequency of a composite genotype involving several loci is the product of the single locus genotype frequencies. This differs from HW proportions in an important way, however. HW proportions are attained in a single generation of random mating, whereas random frequencies at multiple loci are attained only gradually. If the loci are on different (nonhomologous) chromosomes, or far apart on the same chromosome, the approach is rapid; the departure from the final equilibrium is halved each generation. The equilibrium state is called linkage equilibrium (LE).[12]

Empirical studies of large numbers of VNTRs show close agreement with LE for two loci, and with smaller numbers for three loci (some of the data are summarized in NRC 1996, pp. 108–112). Furthermore, departures from LE can be in either direction, so with multiple loci opposite deviations to some extent cancel. Data for STRs are now quite extensive and follow the same population rules as VNTRs. Recent studies (e.g., Lins et al. 1998; Budowle et al. 1999) show good agreement with LE. Although it would be wrong to claim exact linkage equilibrium, current tests on two loci would detect discrepancies that are large enough to alter the conclusion that LE is a suitable approximation for practical forensic work.

Using HW frequencies for each locus and multiplying these frequencies for all loci is known as the **product rule**. It has been widely accepted in the U.S. courts. The NRC 1996 report estimated that the match probabilities from the product rule for VNTRs are likely to be correct within a factor of 10 in either direction (a range of 100 fold). The DNA Advisory Board (DAB 2000) recommends product rule calculations as appropriate approximations for STRs. See also Budowle et al. (1999).

Structured populations. Of course, the U.S. population is not a single randomly mating unit. Within a major group there are subpopulations, with matings more likely to occur within a subpopulation than between subpopulations. On the average the effect of such substructure is to increase the proportion of homozygotes and decrease the proportion of heterozygotes, since people in a subpopulation tend to be somewhat related.

The changes in population proportions due to such substructuring are discussed in appendix A5.1, p. 56.

---

12. This wording is traditionally used even for loci that are unlinked. There are better expressions, but we shall go along with this time-honored verbal infelicity.

If we use Equations (1) to calculate match probabilities, we are implicitly assuming that the two DNA samples (e.g., from the crime scene and from the suspect) are independent. It is likely, however, that they are not completely independent. For example, both may be from the same population subgroup. We shall use θ as a measure of population substructure. Empirical measurements for major U. S populations give θ values less than 0.01 (see table on page 57).

In this case, the appropriate procedure is to use the conditional probabilities corrected for population structure to estimate match probabilities. One widely used formula was originally given by Balding and Nichols (1994) and was recommended by NRC (1996). It was derived on the assumption that the population structure is at equilibrium. With a conservatively chosen value of θ it can also be regarded as a conservative approximation. Other assumptions about the causes of population structure lead to formulae that agree to good approximation when θ is small enough that terms in θ^2 can be neglected (Morton 1992; Crow and Denniston 1993; Roeder 1994). The agreement among formulae based on various assumptions increases our confidence in their broad applicability.

The θ-corrected conditional match probabilities are:

$$P(A_iA_i|A_iA_i) = \frac{[2\theta + (1-\theta)p_i][3\theta + (1-\theta)p_i]}{(1 + \theta)(1 + 2\theta)} \qquad (2a)$$

$$P(A_iA_j|A_iA_j) = \frac{2[\theta + (1-\theta)p_i][\theta + (1-\theta)p_j]}{(1 + \theta)(1 + 2\theta)} \qquad (2b)$$

Notice that, when $\theta = 0$, these are the Hardy-Weinberg formulae.

Current practice varies as to whether, in calculating multiple-locus match probabilities, the conditional probabilities (Equations 2) should be routinely employed (Evett and Weir 1998), or used only when there is reason to believe that the two persons belong to the same subpopulation (NRC 1996, DAB 2000). The difference between Equations (1) and (2) is not large as long as θ is less than 0.01, and using a different formula is unlikely to change the interpretation. (See p. 63.)

Native American populations have a much more structured population, so taking $\theta = 0.03$ is recommended by the DAB.

Laboratory errors. It has been suggested that the probability of a laboratory or chain-of-custody error should be included in calculating the match probability. This was rejected by NRC (1996) on the grounds that these errors are difficult to measure and are likely to change over time as techniques and procedures improve. The committee recommended instead that whenever possible only a part of the evidence material be used for analysis and the rest retained for possible future use. With PCR methods it is very unlikely that the entire evidence DNA is consumed in the analysis. As emphasized in the NRC report, the best protection for a suspect who may have been wrongly accused because of an error is the opportunity for an independent retest.

c. Partial Matches

In the appendix (A5.2, p. 66) we give an example of two STR profiles that share both alleles at six loci, one allele at six, and none at one. Not being identical, these did not come from the same person. But the large proportion of matches of both alleles, which is expected somewhat more than 1/4 of the time in siblings, argues strongly that the two samples came from siblings.

In this particular example, the likelihood ratio for siblings versus unrelated persons is about a million; that is, the match probability is a million times as great if the DNAs came from siblings as if they came from unrelated persons. Furthermore, the match probability is 500 times as great if they came from full sibs as if from half sibs. So there is strong statistical support for the conclusion that they came from full siblings. We have chosen these two profiles as a particularly striking example of a sib pattern. Although these are actual sibs, the large number of matches is unusual. Note that a parent-child relationship can be ruled out, except for the possibility of mutation, since parent and child always share an allele.

We can anticipate more examples of relatives being found as tests include a larger number of loci and as database searches become more common. The legal propriety of identifying relatives in forensic investigations is uncertain and customs differ from State to State.[13]

d. Individualization ("Uniqueness")

As the number of analyzed loci increases, the probability of a second, unrelated person having the same profile becomes ever smaller. Eventually, the probability becomes so small that the profile is effectively unique. The basis for concern would then be whether the techniques are adequate, the chain of custody is intact, the statistical treatment is appropriate, and no errors were made. But how small must such a probability be for a profile to be individualized?

The FBI in 1997 announced a new policy that has been used several times in court cases by the FBI and others and has not been rejected. This assumes that if the match probability is substantially less than the reciprocal of the U. S. population, then it can be stated with "reasonable scientific certainty" that a particular individual is the source of the DNA sample. The procedure is given by Budowle et al. (2000), and DAB (2000) and is described in appendix 5.1c, p. 58.

The statistical basis for individualization is discussed by Evett and Weir (1998, pp. 243–244). The concept of individualization has been supported by Balding (1999). The FBI procedure has been criticized by Weir (1999) and supported by Budowle, Chakraborty, et al. (2000). Whether this, or in fact any statistical procedure for defining individualization is

---

13. Although brothers and twins are rare in databases, they can be common among those pairs that are found by profile matching. John Buckleton (2000 personal communication) found that, among ten 6-locus matches in a New Zealand database of 10,907 records, all but 2 were brothers (including twins). This shows that the possibility of sibs cannot be ignored in database searches. We should note, however, that these could usually be identified as brothers, either by further investigation or by testing additional loci.

defensible continues to be debated. The procedure provides one way to interpret discriminatory power (a scientific question) in terms of "a reasonable degree of scientific certainty" (a subjective question). It is quite possible that within 5 years or less some such criterion will be accepted by the legal and forensic community, not as a scientifically appropriate statement, but as a practical definition for forensic purposes.

e. Suspect Identified by Database Search

As discussed above, in traditional forensic analysis one computes the probability, P, of finding in an unrelated person a particular profile matching that of the evidence, E. But if several DNA samples are examined instead of a single suspect, the probability of finding the matching profile is increased correspondingly.

To deal with this problem, the first National Academy of Sciences Committee (NRC 1992) recommended that the information employed in the database search be used for identification of a suspect, but not for evidence in the court. For this purpose use of a separate set of loci was recommended. The observations on the second set obviously do not depend on the manner in which the suspect was found and cannot be biased by it.

The second committee (NRC 1996) agreed with this procedure. However, because of the limited number of VNTR loci then available, it feared that there might not be enough loci left after using some for identification to provide an effective test. In this case the committee noted that, assuming that the source of the evidence was not in the database searched, the probability of one or more profiles in the database matching the evidence profile is $M = 1 - (1-P)^N$. The committee therefore recommended that the match probability be adjusted by this formula. If NP is much less than one, $M \approx NP$.

It should be emphasized that neither NRC committee was considering a database of convicted felons. A random population database was assumed so that a person in the database was no more likely to be the source of the evidence DNA than a random member of the population. It was further assumed that the person contributing the evidence DNA was not in the database.

At present, database searches usually involve convicted felons. Clearly, because of recidivism, a person in the database has a greater probability of being the source than a random member of the population. Therefore, the NRC (1996) recommendation is conservative and is endorsed as such by DAB (2000).

Recently there has been more emphasis in the statistical literature on the likelihood ratio approach. This is discussed in appendix 5.1d, p. 59.

f. Looking to the Future

It is likely that the 13 core STR loci will remain as the standard for some time. This is especially likely for databases. Once these get set up it will be troublesome and expensive to change them. On the other hand, new loci are being discovered constantly. In the near future it will be relatively easy to have 20 or more STR loci, although it is not necessary in most cases.

The day when a DNA profile match is regarded as conclusive is not here yet. One interim approach, before the time when consideration of such things as population structure become unnecessary, is to calculate match probabilities for the closest relatives. If the probability is low, then it will be even lower for any less closely related persons. The closest relatives from this standpoint (except for identical twins) are full sibs. These can be used as a limiting case. In the appendix (A5.1b, p. 57) we give procedures for computing match probabilities for sibs.

It is already apparent that most of the STR variability is within groups. Although groups differ, the mean differences between groups are less than the individual differences within groups; profiles that are rare in one group tend to be rare in others. With enough loci it may be possible to have a single database for all the major groups in the United States. One suggested approach is to use a composite database for the large population groups in the United States: Caucasian Americans, Hispanic Americans, African Americans, and Asian Americans, and then use a larger value of θ. One study gave a value of 0.028 (Chakraborty 2000 personal communication). These are worldwide data; values in the United States should be less because of admixture. Using 0.03 should be appropriately conservative. This may appeal to those who would like to emphasize individual differences and ignore group differences.

8.   Technology Projections

In this section we attempt to foresee what major developments will impact forensic analysis in the next decade. Needless to say, such forecasts are highly uncertain. A look at the past shows us that projections into the future have often been far off. Part of the reason is that unexpected new technologies, such as PCR in the past and, more recently, sequencing chips, came as surprises. So what follows are guesses, but they are informed guesses based on the present state of the art.

a.   Technology Projections for 2002

We clearly foresee that the CODIS 13 STR core-locus set will dominate database applications in this time period. We anticipate that more than 500,000 profiles based on these loci will be included in the national felon database by the year 2002. Fluorescent detection, multiplex systems, and the means for high throughput analysis of the profiles are already available. In addition, more loci have been and will be developed, so many laboratories will have available 20 or more STR loci when needed for special applications.

Allele frequencies for all 13 STR loci are currently published (e.g., Lins et al. 1998, Budowle et al. 1999) and are available electronically. We expect increasing use of these data for calculations of statistical evidence. We anticipate a shift by forensic laboratories away from all other previously used systems, VNTRs in particular, and toward the use of the standard 13 core STR loci. We expect that the frequencies for the STR loci in additional populations and subpopulations will be published and made readily available to all laboratories as new data appear. Likewise, the best estimates of θ (as a measure of population subdivision) should also be on the record. The FBI has coordinated an extensive multilaboratory study and expects to provide a comprehensive publicly available source for these data. These data are now on the World Wide Web. Although the emphasis will be on STRs, some laboratories may prefer for casework to retain their existing markers.[14]

In the near future, significant progress is also expected in the development of specific marker sets that may aid the investigative process beyond identification as currently practiced. Currently, CODIS STR core loci provide information derived from the different allele frequencies present in different population groups. Statistical analysis will allow some level of confidence in determining the group character of the source of stain material. We can also expect progress in discovery of non-STR markers for individual traits.

Mitochondrial DNA markers, which trace maternal lineages, and Y chromosome markers, which trace paternal lineages, will become more numerous and more fully characterized during this period. In fact, the region of mtDNA with the richest sequence polymorphism (the control region) is already defined. Because all mitochondrial loci are completely linked, the power to determine the significance of a match depends on the size of data-bases characterizing them. These database sizes, and the corresponding power of the systems, are expected to increase significantly during the next 2 years. The greatest strength of mtDNA is its great sensitivity. Amounts of DNA that would be too small to be used for chromosomal markers can often be analyzed by mtDNA. We therefore expect greater use of mtDNA for marginal cases, e.g., DNA that is badly degraded or available in very tiny amounts. Y chromosome and mtDNA haplotypes are currently employed mainly to establish a relationship of sample material among family members in the absence of the individual suspected of leaving the sample. They may be used to provide information for group identification.

We also expect to see improvements in techniques for collection of evidence, isolation of DNA, and quantification of the DNA during the next 2 years. Processes that simplify these procedures are being developed. Improvements are expected in automation and minia-turization that should allow more rapid processing of larger numbers of samples.

Ehrlich and his associates (Schmalzing et al. 1998, 1999) have developed a miniaturized system for analyzing STRs. They currently report a laser-induced fluorescence detection system that can do a quick analysis of eight of the CORE loci. With a resolution of four bases, the process can be completed in 2 minutes. Resolution to one base requires about 10 minutes. The device is about 150 mm in diameter and made from fused-silica wafers. At present, this is in the experimental stage. It should be ready for some operations by the end of this period. This, and similar developments in other laboratories, will permit much more rapid analysis and make possible processing larger numbers of samples. We expect further progress in miniaturization and portability.

---

14. A problem in the recent past has been the reluctance of journals to publish data on STR frequencies, on the reasonable grounds that these do not represent new concepts. In November 1999, the *Journal of Forensic Sciences* adopted a brief format for publishing data in standard form. This presents the minimum information in compact form, usually allele frequencies. The data are published on the assumption that the complete data set is available on the Web or will be provided on request. This should go a long way toward relieving the publishing problem and making the rapidly growing body of data more readily available.

We can expect to have more cases of postconviction analysis. As of now, more than 70 prisoners have been released by such analysis. There are also pre-DNA cases that are as yet unresolved. These do not require a large number of markers; usually only a few are sufficient to establish a nonmatch. For this reason, well-established systems that are inexpensive and robust and have been used for years, such as DQA/polymarker/D1S80, will continue to be useful, especially in initial investigations where they can provide rapid exoneration when the profiles do not match.

b. Technology Projections for 2005

We expect full establishment of the CODIS database within this time period with more than 1.5 million profiles present and general use in crime analysis in essentially all States, with cooperation among them. Developed procedures for investigating potential of international matches are also expected, especially with Britain, where there is a well-developed convicted felon database. Eight of the STR loci routinely used in the United Kingdom are included within the 13 core loci, so meaningful comparisons are possible (and are occasionally carried out).

In 5 years, the sequence determination of the Human Genome Project essentially will be completed. A first draft, representing about 90-percent completion, was announced in June 2000. This program will generate a host of new potential markers as well as new techniques for high-throughput evaluation of current and new markers.

A dynamic interplay will be seen in maintaining uniformity in the genetic markers used in the national database versus the improved performance or efficiency of new markers for particular applications. Crime laboratories around the country will have standardized on the CODIS 13 loci, leading to the prediction that this marker set will remain as a standard for database analysis during this period.

The genetic markers employed as the STR core of the national databases are expected to be quite stable during this period. Many laboratories will be equipped for mtDNA, which is expected to be useful for maternal lineages and in circumstances in which the DNA is too limited or degraded for other systems. Tests employed for applications beyond the identity determination itself may be influenced by information from the Human Genome Project. Beyond the use of additional STR and mtDNA loci, SNPs and Alu markers are expected to be well defined for use in determination of ancestral geographic origin. SNPs will be useful as another tool for analysis of degraded samples in which the fragments are too small for STR. Some use of additional genetic markers for investigative purposes will probably occur within this period.

In 5 years, we expect laboratory procedures to be largely automated and for computerized analysis to be commonplace. Even now, systems have been developed that provide automatic profiling to confirm results determined by a human user. As the rules of determining alleles continue to be refined and the reliability of these expert systems is improved and confirmed, they will take on a greater role in the preliminary evaluations of matches. These timesaving approaches are not expected to replace human judgments in the final review of data. However, automation of many of the more routine aspects of analysis is expected to yield significant cost savings.

Beyond the use of expert systems for match determination, these computer-based analyses are expected to provide improved information regarding the possible components of samples containing more than one DNA source. Another example of implementation of these systems is the calculation of the level of statistical confidence that a DNA sample is derived from a donor descended from a particular ancestral geographic origin.

While the genetic markers used in database searching are expected to remain fairly constant over this time period, the means to analyze them are undergoing a revolution. In particular, the use of "chips" is expected to find limited usage in this time period. This is the name given to processes that involve photolithography and chemical etching techniques similar to those used in the manufacture of microelectronic chips.

The chip formats (see appendix A4.f, p. 53) expected to be most easily adapted to the general evaluation of the core STR loci are those that use etching techniques in combination with electrokinetic forces to miniaturize several common laboratory techniques central to the current DNA analyses. These techniques include the polymerase chain reaction, capillary electrophoresis, DNA sequencing, and STR fragment detection and analysis. Chip technology that is focused on supporting existing analytical methods and genetic markers is expected to be adapted readily to existing database systems.

As mentioned earlier, one laboratory has developed a circular chip about 6 inches in diameter that can analyze eight STR loci in a few minutes (Schmalzing et al. 1999). Such devices should be available within the 5-year period. Perhaps in the 5-year period and much more likely within 10 years, there will be handheld, portable units that can do a DNA analysis for the 13 core STR loci in a few minutes right at the crime scene. We note, however, that developing something that works reasonably well in a research laboratory is quite different from having it reliable enough for forensic use.

A second format, hybridization array analysis, is based primarily on photolithography and spotting, as mentioned above. In this approach, DNA sequences are attached directly to a solid surface and act as probes to hybridize with sample material or amplified labeled sample material. The general approach is similar to the reverse dot blot method. Because high-density arrays can be generated in this process, many loci or sequences in an individual sample can be analyzed simultaneously. However, because the arrays are predefined, incorporation of new variants and new loci into the assay requires manufacture of new chips.

The forecast of timing for implementation of reliable and validated chip formats in forensic use is currently uncertain. Whether these formats will proceed to full implementation in this time period is unknown, but the efforts in progress to develop multiple alternatives at present assures that some options for testing and validation will become available within this 5-year period.

The trend toward increasing automation will continue. So will the move toward miniaturization. This course will be strongly influenced by the research and medical diagnostics communities. The time of transition to validated use within the forensic community will be driven primarily by identification of specifically needed applications rather than by technology development in this area.

c. Technology Projections for 2010

In this time period, a variety of genetic systems will be used, including STRs, SNPs, and direct automated DNA sequence analysis. Beyond the use of these markers for direct identification comparisons, markers are expected to exist for determination of a variety of physical characteristics of suspects based on biological samples left at crime scenes. These could include facial features, skin, hair and eye color, propensity for genetic diseases or abnormalities, a partial history of infectious disease (including genetic remnants of parasites or genetic determination of individual antibody profiles), and expected range of height and weight.

We can expect multiplex amplification of a large number of loci to be possible. This will make possible the addition of additional STR loci and probably a large number of SNPs.

The miniaturization of processes associated with DNA analysis will lead to the ability to use transportable devices capable of much of the analysis. The improvements in automation of both analysis and interpretation will mean that workers will be spared some routine tasks and can concentrate on higher functions. These improvements in conjunction with advances in communications technology will allow investigators to consider testing DNA samples at the crime scene with remote links to databases or sources of expertise. Such a prompt determination of the profile at the crime scene could speed the identification of a suspect or the elimination of innocent persons from erroneous consideration. Miniaturized, rapid, portable, handheld chips may be in use in 10 years.

Movement away from the use of STR loci for database use cannot be predicted with any certainty. The use of databases depends fundamentally upon profile determinations using the same genetic markers in the database as those with the crime scene materials. As alternative methods of analysis are refined, the cost of moving to the new system must be weighed against the cost of abandoning and replacing the existing database and the national technical and legal infrastructure supporting it. Should such a change be implemented, it is anticipated that the older and the newer technologies would be employed together in the database for some period of time to allow for this adjustment to occur.

On the other hand, improvements in methods to collect evidence, and to simplify, accelerate, and lower the cost of analysis of the chosen genetic markers are not limited by the choice of standardization on core STR loci in the database. In addition, genetic tests based on new sequence-based polymorphisms, such as SNPs, may be introduced. These may be more effective and less affected by degraded DNA than STRs. With the human genome project and its myriad of applications driving this process, this area is expected to explode with growth and technological improvement. A great deal will depend on the extent to which CODIS is used effectively; this can accelerate improvements in STR technology.

By this time there should be enough markers to distinguish between any two individuals, including close relatives, with very high likelihood. Perhaps we shall have a socially or court-approved consensus as to what constitutes a unique identification. It is also probable that, in cases where it is necessary, identical twins may be distinguished.

We summarize the material of the past sections in tabular form on the following pages.

d. Summarizing Charts: Chronological Projections of Technology and Population Advances

Item	Next 2 Years (Year 2002)	5 Years (Approximately Year 2005)	10 Years (Approximately Year 2010)
	Technology Issues		
1	Shift from VNTRs to CODIS 13 STR Systems using fluorescent detection of multiplex systems. Continuation of DQA-A/polymarker/D1S80 systems for rapid analysis.	CODIS STR Database established. Higher throughput approaches will eliminate backlog of tests. Automation of STR analysis. Miniaturization of STR analysis. More rapid STR analysis. Routine procedures for international database comparison in place.	Possible, but not certain, database transition to new technology. Drive to shift genetic markers requires major improvements in convenience or cost. Possibly single nucleotide polymorphisms (SNPs) in conjunction with automation and miniaturization technology (driven by molecular diagnostics applications). Database use benefits from conservation of type of information (i.e., genetic profiles) stored. Should a change occur, a period of overlap in use of two technologies is envisioned.
2	Additional STR loci beyond CODIS core available for casework analyses.	Still more STR loci available.	
3	Increased development of mtDNA for situations where great sensitivity is required. Increased database size.	Further increase in mtDNA database size.	
4	Increased interest in Y chromosome markers for ethnology grouping and for resolving sexual assault mixtures.	Wider use of Y chromosome and other markers (e.g., Alu) for ancestral geographical origin. Increased population database size	
5	Availability of other markers to determine the ancestral geographic origin of individuals.	Establishment of profiles for some physical characteristics and determination of ancestral geographic origin.	General physical characteristic markers for investigative purposes.
6	More emphasis on collection and purification techniques.	Establishment of improved sample storage media.	

continued on next page

d. Summarizing Charts: Chronological Projections of Technology and Population Advances *(continued)*

Item	Next 2 Years (Year 2002)	5 Years (Approximately Year 2005)	10 Years (Approximately Year 2010)
	Technology Issues		
7		Human genome and clinical research provide many new potential markers and analytical techniques to consider for forensic use.	Human genome and clinical research provide crime scene instrumentation with computer-linked remote analysis.
8	Improved interpretation software—STR profiling, mixture analysis, etc.	Increased integration of computers and INTERNET with analytical techniques.	Crime scene instrument for sample handling with links to remote sites of analysis.
	Population Issues		
9	Definition/recommendations for statistical interpretation of mtDNA and Y chromosome markers.		
10	Possible access to CODIS databases for statistical analyses and quality assurance related to forensic purposes.	Agreement to use or not to use CODIS databases for statistical studies beyond forensic use.	
11	Greater development of computer-based statistical interpretation of mixed samples.	Greater development of computer-based statistical interpretation of ancestral geographic origin.	
12	Ability to discriminate siblings with a high degree of confidence.		In most cases, a unique profile for each person.
13	Continued discussion and partial implementation of use of the concept of uniqueness (individualization).	General agreement on a practical working definition of uniqueness.	
14	Continued discussion of guidelines regarding the effect of database size on statistical evaluation of a database hit.	General agreement on appropriate consideration of database identification of suspect and accompanying statistical analysis for casework.	

9. Some Other Technology Issues

There seems to be little need for a recommendation from our group about developing new systems and improving existing ones. Private laboratories, Federal departments, and universities are aggressively researching new techniques. These advances will occur, driven by competition among laboratories and researchers and the development of new techniques for medical and other uses. But they will be quickly adapted to forensic applications only if there is financial support. Much of what has been learned and developed in the past has been done with the aid of Federal funds. It will be important to continue Federal support for development of forensic applications, since the commercial market is small and this means slower technology transfer to forensic applications.

We make a confident prediction that the CODIS core STR loci will be used throughout this period. The CODIS database and the State-sponsored support for it are expensive to set up and maintain. Laboratories will have invested heavily in equipment, training, and generation of genetic profiles. They have every reason to expect that the system will be stable. On the other hand, methods to reveal these genetic profiles more rapidly or inexpensively will flourish and compete for prominence.

What does that say about newer and undoubtedly better methods that will have been developed? In the near future there will be ways of making STR analysis more efficient—automation, miniaturization, robotics, greater speed, etc. These can be used to improve the efficiency of analysis of the 13 core loci as well as to augment the number of loci. In addition to database development, a variety of genetic markers will find special applications in cases requiring information on family lineage, difficult samples, and investigative problems.

Several times in the past, legal issues have involved DNA analysis of animals and plants (Kaye and Sensabaugh 2000). We can expect data generated in ongoing nonhuman genome projects to facilitate the expanded use of this approach. This must be accompanied by appropriate methods of validation to establish the value of the approaches. Much of the useful information in these cases will probably come from genes for specific traits.

As methods based on DNA sequence become more and more effective, each individual animal will have an effectively unique profile, even in highly inbred species. This should apply in many cases to plants and microorganisms as well. It may well be, in 10 years or less, that the bacterial, protozoan, and virus parasites of a person can be analyzed with precision. Each of us has a unique constellation of parasites, and DNA (or RNA) from these may one day provide evidence of identity comparable to the person's own DNA. As mentioned earlier, such methods may lead to the capability of distinguishing between identical twins.

10. Social, Ethical, and Legal Issues

We are aware that a number of issues raised in this report have social, ethical, and legal implications beyond the assignment of the working group. We have no special qualifications for dealing with them. Instead, we identify some of the problems and call them to the attention of the Commission and other groups.

Group and trait identification. We have mentioned that STR allele frequencies differ in different population groups. Thus, a particular profile in a crime scene sample may be more probable in one group than in another. This can be used as a likelihood ratio with appropriate prior probabilities to provide evidence for the group origin of the DNA sample. There are also genes that are common in some groups and rare in others; one Duffy blood group allele is an example. Such information can be of value for crime investigation. Like an eyewitness account it can be helpful in narrowing the search for a suspect. But, also like an eyewitness account, it may be quite unreliable. There are objections on the grounds that classifying possible suspects on ancestral grounds can be interpreted as stigmatizing some groups. There is already much public discussion of "racial profiling." This is not the same, but to some it is too close for comfort.

This is a time of very rapid progress in gene identification, thanks to the Human Genome Project and numerous research laboratories. Genetic markers for eye, hair, and skin color, for color-blindness, for baldness, and for less common traits such as albinism will soon be discovered, if they have not been already. We can expect the number to increase rapidly. We again note that the identification for complex traits will almost always be likelihoods rather than certainties, at least in the near future. But even imprecise information can be useful. We also emphasize that genes used for trait identification are not currently used in ordinary forensic work, with the exception of amelogenin for sex identification. The 13 STR loci, as we have emphasized, are not associated with specific, observable traits. Throughout this report, our emphasis has been on identifying individuals as such, and not as members of groups. Consistent with this view, we emphasize for future development the desirability of markers for traits rather than for groups.

Identification of relatives. With 13 STR loci it is quite likely that a search of a database will identify a person who is a relative of the person contributing the evidence sample. We discussed earlier a pair of profiles that almost certainly came from siblings, and parent-child combinations can also often be identified. Other close relatives may also be identified, but with less certainty (see appendix A5.2b, p. 65). Suppose a crime scene profile shows a partial match with someone in the database. Are law enforcement officers entitled to investigate the relatives? At present, laws in different States are different. In Virginia, for example, this is forbidden.

Broadening the database. The largest database at present is that of convicted felons, usually perpetrators of major crimes. There is considerable interest in increasing the database to include persons convicted of lesser crimes or arrestees. In Britain everyone arrested for offenses that would lead to prison terms if convicted has a DNA sample taken at the time of arrest, but the profile is removed from the database if the person is not convicted. These are issues beyond the responsibilities of this Research and Development Working Group. We note that increasing the database size will increase the number of crimes solved through its use. This benefit will require the inclusion of methods to deal with the changes in the prior odds for a suspect to be found in such a database search.

Inevitably, there will be the increasing possibility of broadening the database to include the general public. There would be many advantages, such as identification of persons or body parts after accidents, or discovery of kidnapped or lost people. At the same time, the risk to individual privacy would be enhanced and protection of anonymity would be harder. Balancing benefits and risks of population databases will continue to be a contentious issue in the future.

Saving DNA samples. At present, there is no clear overall policy as to what happens to the DNA sample after profiles are added to the database, but the majority of States now have sample storage policies. It can be argued that saving the DNA permits retesting and inclusion of additional loci, particularly newly discovered ones. This would be much more efficient than searching out the person, who may not even be living. On the other side, it is argued that the profiles are recorded and that this information is all that is needed, not the DNA itself. Furthermore, those fearful of invasion of privacy are concerned lest the DNA become available to unauthorized parties or otherwise be used in ways that would disclose information that ought to remain confidential.

Use of CODIS database for research. As the database enlarges and if it is broadened to include persons convicted of a larger variety of crimes, it might be possible that statistical studies of the databases could reveal useful information. Inventive researchers may glean useful information of a statistical sort. At the same time, there would need to be protection against misuse or use by unauthorized persons.

Our assignment is to study technological issues. So, although we have tried to provide information, the discussion of these various issues has ramifications that should be treated by a more widely representative group.

III. Appendix: Technical Summaries

A1. Genetic Markers Based on Repeat Sequences

a. Variable Number of Tandem Repeats (VNTRs)

VNTRs, a type of RFLP (restriction fragment length polymorphism), are regions of DNA comprising a thousand to several thousand base pairs. These are not genes, for they produce no product, which means that they are not responsible for any observable genetic traits. A typical VNTR is made up of a large number of tandemly repeated units. The size of the repeat unit in different VNTRs used for forensic analysis varies from 8 to 80 base pairs (usually 15 to 35). Although the unit size is nearly constant at a given VNTR locus, the number of repeats is highly variable, so that there are sometimes a hundred or more different lengths observed in different persons. It is this great variability in length that makes VNTRs so useful for forensic analysis.

The technique for determining the length of a particular VNTR is simple in principle. The DNA is first extracted from whatever material is to be analyzed. It is then treated with an enzyme that cuts the DNA at every point where a specific base sequence occurs. For example, the enzyme *Hae* III finds the sequence GGCC (CCGG on the opposite strand) and cuts both strands between G and C. In this way the DNA is cut into millions of pieces whose sizes are determined by the distance between successive GGCC sequences. The collection of fragments is then placed on a flat gel, which is exposed to an electric field. The fragments migrate at different rates, depending on their size, a process called electrophoresis. The separated fragments are then treated chemically to denature them, that is to separate each fragment into two single strands of complementary base sequence (see A4, a and b, pp. 50–51).

Because gels are somewhat fragile and awkward to handle, the fragments are transferred by direct contact to a nylon membrane, to which they adhere (much as a blotter picks up ink from a paper). Thus, the fragments are located on the membrane in positions congruent with their positions in the gel. The membrane is then flooded with a probe, which is a short, single-stranded piece of DNA that is complementary to a particular fragment among the millions on the membrane. Because of the specific DNA base-pairing rules (A with T and G with C), the probe finds and attaches itself to the appropriate fragment, one in which the complementary bases match those of the probe. Any excess probe that does not bind to a DNA fragment is washed off.

Attached to the probe is a label used to signal its presence. This is detected by a photographic film placed in contact with the nylon membrane. Originally, labels were radioactive atoms, exposing the film at sites corresponding to the probe's position on the membrane. Although radioactive probes are still employed in some settings, luminescent detection is now more commonly employed. The membrane is coated with a material that is converted into light by an enzyme attached to the probe. The light output is captured on film over a period of a few hours. The position of bands visualized in this process is used to characterize the original DNA sample.

Typically, two DNA samples to be compared are run in parallel lanes on the same gel. If the VNTR fragments occupy corresponding positions, they are declared to match. If not, there is a nonmatch and the two DNAs have come from different persons (unless there is an error). A match can mean either that the two DNAs are from the same person or they are from different persons who happen to have VNTR fragments of the same size.

The precision of measurement of fragment sizes is such that VNTR alleles that differ by only one or two repeat units are usually indistinguishable. For this reason the bands of similar size are grouped into **bins**. In this way the total number of alleles is reduced from hundreds to 20 to 30. The frequencies of the alleles that fall into the various bins are published (e.g., FBI 1993 or in the peer-reviewed literature), and in this fashion each VNTR band is assigned a frequency of occurrence corresponding to the bin in which it falls. This frequency is used in calculating the match probability. This is called the **fixed bin** procedure and is the most widely applied. The alternative, **floating bin**, procedure is statistically preferable, but the fixed bin is more commonly used since it is simpler to understand and easier to calculate (NRC 1996, pp. 139–145).

The main reasons why VNTRs have been useful, and still are for some purposes, are their robustness and the large number of alleles per locus. The following table gives some representative information. The first number in the locus designation tells the chromosome location. Loci are chosen to be on different chromosomes or, if on the same chromosome, far apart, so as to be inherited independently. The ideal locus would have a large number of alleles, each with the same frequency. The data fall short of this ideal, of course. The most informative simple number to measure the discriminating power of a locus is the heterozygosity. This is computed from the allele frequencies, assuming Hardy-Weinberg proportions. More useful is the population match probability, the probability that two randomly chosen genotypes will be the same (for method of calculation, see A5, Equation A2, p. 62). The data below are for a Caucasian American sample.

Table A1. *Number of alleles, average heterozygosity, and population match probability for random pairs in the Caucasian American population for six VNTR loci.*

Locus	No. bins	Heterozygosity	Pop. match prob.
D1S7	28	0.945	0.0058
D2S44	26	0.926	0.0103
D4S139	19	0.899	0.0184
D10S28	24	0.943	0.0063
D14S13	30	0.899	0.0172
D17S79	19	0.799	0.0700
Average or product		0.902	8.26×10^{-12} or one in 1.2×10^{11}

Data are from the FBI, 1993.
Similar data are available for other population groups.

The advantages of VNTRs are:

1. There are a large number of alternative forms (bins), 20 to 30 at each locus. The heterozygosity is large. This provides a great deal of discriminatory power per locus.

2. The techniques are well established, are familiar, and have been widely used.

3. These tests are widely accepted by the legal community.

4. The large number of alleles facilitates mixed-sample analysis.

The limitations are:

1. The sensitivity of the technique is limited. Generally 50 ng or more of DNA material is required to obtain clear results.

2. The process is time consuming, taking several days to complete (or weeks if radioactive probes are used).

3. The number of validated loci are limited.

4. Large RFLP fragments are not suitable for use with degraded DNA samples such as are sometimes found in forensic work.

5. The necessity of binning introduces statistical complications and sometimes difficulties of interpretation.

6. Because of the small number of validated loci, VNTRs are of limited value in distinguishing between siblings (see discussion of population issues below).

The most important disadvantage is that, because of their large size, most VNTRs cannot be amplified reliably and consistently by the polymerase chain reaction (PCR) (Saiki et al. 1985; Mullis and Faloona 1987; Saiki et al. 1988). (See appendix 4.c, p.51). Other systems to be discussed take advantage of this technique and therefore can process much smaller amounts of DNA in much less time. This may not be a permanent limitation, however, since a new technique (Richie et al. 1999) permits larger DNA pieces to be amplified. The technique uses a mixture of Taq polymerase and a thermostable proofreading poly- merase. There are still limitations to be overcome: (1) The target genomic DNA is suscep- tible to degradation, and (2) preferential amplification of the smaller allele could cause some heterozygotes to be classified as homozygotes.

b.   Short Tandem Repeats (STRs)

STRs are similar to VNTRs and the general principles for using them are the same. They differ from VNTRs in having smaller repeat units, from 2 to 7 bases, and the total size of a STR is smaller, usually less than 500 bases. The smaller size means that the PCR can be used to amplify very small amounts, less than 1 ng, of DNA. It also permits analysis of degraded DNA, that is DNA that is broken into short pieces. Such degraded DNA often cannot be analyzed by Southern blot analysis of VNTRs, which requires higher quality DNA (e.g., larger fragments). The use of the PCR permits a very tiny amount of DNA, such as would be found on a postage stamp, cigarette butt, or coffee cup, to be amplified to produce an amount large enough to be analyzed. The PCR also consumes less sample, preserving more material for repeat or referee analysis (see A4.c, p. 51)

The amplified products are separated by electrophoresis as described for the VNTR fragments. But, whereas for VNTRs all the DNA in the cells is on the gel, with STRs only the region of interest is amplified. However, the smaller range of fragment sizes of STRs and the use of more discriminating separation systems allow identification of all alleles at a locus. Thus, the requirement for bins is eliminated. There are, however, micro-variants (i.e., alleles that differ from other alleles by less than one repeat length) which increase discriminating power of the system, but can create problems of band resolution.

In forensic applications, amplified and separated STR fragments are generally detected using one of two methods. One method uses the propensity of silver to bind to DNA. The entire gel is stained with silver, but because of the greater amount of DNA in amplified fragments, they stand out against the more dilute background. A second, increasingly prevalent method requires that some of the primers used during the amplification contain fluorescent tags which are incorporated into the STR fragments generated during amplification. Following fragment separation by electrophoresis, an instrument is used to detect the position of separated fluorescent products. Increasingly, laboratories are using real-time detection during electrophoresis. As in the case of the VNTR systems, the sizes (i.e., number of DNA bases) of the STR fragments detected are used to characterize the sample DNA. The allele designation for each locus is generally the number of times a repeated unit is present within the identified fragments.

STR loci that have been selected for forensic uses generally have 7 to 30 different alleles. The population heterozygosity is about 80 percent compared to 90 percent or more for VNTRs. This relatively small number of alleles compared to the VNTR loci usually leads to unambiguous results, but limits the amount of statistical information and significance that can be obtained from an individual locus.

STR loci are very numerous in the genome and many appropriate loci have already been identified. Fortunately, it is possible to analyze a DNA sample at many STR loci simultaneously. Such systems (multiplexes) have been developed that allow amplification of 3 to 16 loci at once. Many forensic laboratories now have instruments that distinguish different fluorescent dyes used to tag particular loci. These advances have allowed the development of multiplex systems that maintain small amplification product sizes, and therefore can use existing separation methods.

The FBI has designated 13 specific STR loci as a core set to be used in matching crime scene materials to previously typed individuals. These loci and their statistical properties for Caucasian American and African American populations are given in table A2.

Table A2. *Number of alleles, heterozygosity, and population match probability in a Caucasian American and African American sample for the 13 CODIS loci.*

Locus	No alleles	Caucasian American		African American	
		Het.	Pop. match pr.	Het.	Pop. match pr.
CSF1PO	11	0.734	0.112	0.781	0.081
TPOX	7	0.621	0.195	0.763	0.090
TH01	7	0.783	0.081	0.727	0.109
vWA	10	0.811	0.062	0.809	0.063
D16S539	8	0.767	0.089	0.798	0.070
D7S820	11	0.806	0.065	0.782	0.080
D13S317	8	0.771	0.085	0.688	0.136
D5S818	10	0.682	0.158	0.739	0.112
FGA	19	0.860	0.036	0.863	0.033
D3S1358	10	0.795	0.075	0.763	0.094
D8S1179	10	0.780	0.067	0.778	0.082
D18S51	15	0.876	0.028	0.873	0.029
D2S11	20	0.853	0.039	0.861	0.034
Average		0.7812		0.7866	
Product			1.738×10^{-15}		1.092×10^{-15}
One in			5.753×10^{14}		9.161×10^{14}

Data are from the FBI.

Comparison with the VNTR data shows that the 13 CODIS loci are somewhat more discriminating than the 6 VNTR loci listed in table A1.

The advantages of STRs are:

1. The process can be used with degraded samples (since shorter fragments of DNA can be analyzed).

2. The PCR process permits analysis of extremely small amounts of DNA.

3. The potential number of loci is very large. This is particularly important if siblings or other relatives are involved.

4. The process is rapid; it may be completed in a day or two.

5. The system lends itself to multiplexing and automation.

6. Kits are available, and for some multiplexes inexpensive silver stain materials may be employed without expensive equipment.

The limitations are:

1. There are a smaller number of alleles and less heterozygosity per locus, so there is less discriminating power per locus than VNTRs.

2. The possibility of contamination from stray DNA is increased because of the amplification process.

3. The equipment is relatively expensive if high-throughput analysis of fluorescently labeled multiplex systems are used. Silver stain STR systems require less investment, but the number of loci in a single system is limited (usually to no more than three per multiplex).

4. "Stutter bands" and unbalanced peak heights may occur and make the interpretation of mixtures more difficult.

c. Pentanucleotide Repeats

These regions of DNA are a subset of the STRs, described above. Pentanucleotide repeats are characterized by repeating units five bases long. They were isolated and developed because they offer a sharper amplification product with fewer "stutter bands" than other classes of STR loci. In particular, STR loci with two, three, or four base repeats generate the identifying band, which is the designated allele, plus one or more fragments one repeat unit larger or smaller (or both) than the designated allele. These bands, often called stutter bands, are less prevalent with systems containing larger repeat units, and the identification of loci containing five base repeats can often nearly eliminate stutter bands. It is anticipated that improvements in methodology may also reduce or eliminate stutter in the CORE 13 loci, making them still more effective.

The products generated by STR loci containing four base repeats are sufficient for general forensic use. However, the improved purity of pentanucleotide amplification products leads to less ambiguity in analysis, especially with DNA mixtures such as those that commonly occur in rape cases and with mixed blood stains. With the pentanucleotide systems, there is less opportunity to confuse a stutter band with the contribution of a second source of DNA.

Pentanucleotide repeat loci are present in the human genome in much smaller numbers than loci containing smaller repeat units. However, several highly discriminating loci with 14 to 24 alleles each have been identified and characterized to date.

The advantages of pentanucleotides are:

1. In general, these have the same advantages as other STRs. In addition:

2. Cleaner amplification with fewer artifacts allows simpler and more precise interpretation of results because of a lower percentage of stutter band artifacts.

3. Some pentanucleotide loci display a high degree of heterozygosity without a significant number of microvariants.

4. Longer repeat length and a paucity of microvariants provides more flexibility in separation technique by allowing interpretation following less extensive separation of amplified products.

5. Preliminary population studies indicate that some pentanucleotide repeats may offer increased ability to determine the racial origin of a DNA sample.

The limitations are:

1. In general, the disadvantages are the same as those of other STRs.

2. These are rare in the genome, compared to shorter repeats.

A2. Genetic Markers Based on Nucleotide Site Polymorphisms

a. Single Nucleotide Polymorphisms (SNPs)

Single nucleotide polymorphisms represent alterations in DNA sequence at a single nucleotide position, whether due to base changes or to insertion or deletion of one or a few bases. The means to detect these alterations and the number of such known polymorphisms has changed dramatically in recent years.

The first SNPs were detected in the 1960s. For example, different serological markers used in early forensic analyses are fundamentally due to collections of individual DNA sequence alterations. With the advent of the use of restriction endonucleases to digest DNA and the use of Southern hybridization (see below) for detection, it was discovered that DNA alterations could be detected by loss or gain of a restriction site. A large number of these restriction fragment length polymorphisms (RFLPs) were used to generate the first full genetic linkage map in humans.

More recently, with the increased use of direct sequence determination of amplified segments of DNA, sequence variation is detected throughout the genome without the limited ascertainment of restriction endonucleases. Base variations are observed, on average, every 1,000 bases throughout the genome. Generally speaking, SNPs are bi-allelic, but may contain three or four alleles. While single loci are limited in their discrimination value because of the limited number of alleles, vast numbers of these loci exist and are being cataloged at a rapid rate.

While DNA sequence analysis is still relatively cumbersome today, SNP analysis may be performed by a variety of simpler and more rapid methods such as the dot-blot format using labeled sequence-specific oligonucleotide (SSO) hybridization, reverse dot blot analysis (see below), and hybridization array technologies (see chip technologies, A4, p. 53).

The advantages of SNPs are:

1. These markers are very numerous in mammalian genomes.

2. Many methods of SNP detection are available.

3. The amplification of alleles is not prone to preferential amplification and robust multiplex amplification is relatively easy to achieve.

The limitations are:

1. Most SNPs are bi-allelic. Even those sites with three alleles are individually of limited discriminatory value.

2. The small number of alleles complicates the analysis of mixed samples.

b. HLA-DQA1

The initial forensic application of PCR-based genetic typing in 1986 used the SSO (sequence specific oligonucleotide) method to analyze single nucleotide polymorphisms at the *HLA-DQA1* (initially termed DQ-α) locus on chromosome 6 (6p21.3). The first commercial PCR test was based on hybridization of a labeled PCR product, amplified from the second exon of the *HLA-DQA1* locus, to an immobilized array of SSO probes on a nylon strip. This format is known as the reverse dot-blot or reverse line-blot, depending on whether the probes are deposited on the nylon membrane as dots or as lines. It is called "reverse" blot because, in contrast to Southern blot analysis of VNTRs, it is the probe, rather than the target DNA being analyzed, that is fixed to the membrane.

The current procedure uses 11 probes, which distinguish 7 allele groups. The PCR product is labeled during the PCR amplification by using primers that have been conjugated to biotin. Following denaturation of the PCR product (the separation of the two DNA strands), the biotinylated strands are hybridized to the immobilized probe array. The presence of the PCR product bound to a specific probe is detected using a biotin-binding molecule, streptavidin conjugated to the enzyme horseradish peroxidase (SA-HRP). The horseradish peroxidase converts a colorless soluble substrate into a blue precipitate, thus producing a blue dot.

The average heterozygosity of the 7 allele system is 0.828. The probability of identity of two randomly chosen persons is about 0.053. Since an average of 95 percent of those wrongly accused can be eliminated by this system, it is particularly useful as a preliminary test to quickly clear innocent suspects.

c. Polymarker (PM)

Additional genetic markers using the reverse dot-blot format have been commercially available since 1993. In this test, primer pairs for five loci (LDLR, GYPA, HBGG, D7S8, and GC), in addition to the HLA-DQA1 primers, are used to co-amplify these six loci. Three of these loci have two alleles, distinguishable by two probes and two loci have three alleles, distinguishable by three probes. Thus, in one PCR and one hybridization reaction with two immobilized probe arrays, the DQA1 strip and the PM strip, genotypes at six loci can be determined. Assuming statistical independence of the alleles at these loci, the frequency of a given six locus genotype can be estimated by multiplying the population frequencies for the single locus genotypes (the product rule). Instruments are available for automating the strip hybridization, wash, and color development for these immobilized probe array assays.

The properties of the HLA-DQA1 plus polymarker loci for the Caucasian American population are in table A3.

Table A3. *Forensic properties of HLA-polymarker system.*

Locus	No. bins	Heterozygosity	Pop. match prob.
DQA1	7	0.828	0.053
LDLR	2	0.493	0.379
GYPA	2	0.498	0.376
HBGG	3	0.508	0.360
D7S8	2	0.476	0.388
GC	3	0.592	0.235
Av. or product		0.566	0.00025 or one in 4,000

Advantages:

1. The method is quick and simple and the results can be interpreted visually. There is no requirement for instrumentation after PCR amplification.

2. It is familiar and has been widely used.

3. It uses PCR methods, so it is capable of analyzing small or degraded samples.

Limitations:

1. Since the number of alleles and developed loci are small, the current system lacks the discriminating power of VNTRs and STRs.

2. The limited number of alleles per locus makes identification of components of mixtures more difficult than with VNTR and STR loci.

d. Alu Sequences (Insertion Polymorphisms)

The study of human population genetics and forensics has involved the analysis of a number of different nuclear and mitochondrial markers. The insertion of mobile genetic elements into the genome represents an alternative source for the study of human genomic diversity in which the ancestral state of each polymorphism is known and the individual alleles are identical by descent. The Alu family of short interspersed elements (SINEs) is distributed throughout the genomes of primates and is the most abundant class of mobile elements within the human genome. Alu elements have amplified as a repeated DNA sequence family in the last 65 million years of primate evolution and are thought to have been spread throughout the genome via an RNA-mediated transposition process (retroposition). Alu sequences have dispersed throughout the human genome in an ongoing process during different evolutionary time periods resulting in the expansion of subfamilies of Alu repeats of different genetic ages. The most recently formed subfamilies of Alu sequences have been termed Y, Ya5, Ya8, and Yb8.

Many of the young (Ya5/8 and Yb8) Alu insertions are so recent in origin that they are polymorphic for presence or absence in the present human population. Alu insertion polymorphisms offer several advantages over other nuclear DNA polymorphisms for forensic studies. First, they are typed by rapid, simple, PCR-based assays; second, they are stable structures that rarely undergo deletions; third, the presence of an Alu element represents identity by descent since the probability that different young Alu repeats would integrate independently into the same chromosomal location is negligible; fourth, the ancestral state is known to be the absence of an Alu element, which can be used to root trees of population relationship; fifth, some of these loci have population-specific alleles with large differences in allele frequencies between diverse populations. All of these properties enhance the forensic utility of Alu elements, and these properties also apply to other mobile elements within the human genome such as long interspersed elements (LINEs) or L1 elements that are also currently expanding within the human genome.

The ongoing mobilization and hierarchical subfamily structure of Alu and L1 mobile elements within the human genome presents the opportunity for the identification of Alu and L1 elements that display large differences in allele frequency between individuals with different geographic affiliation. The analysis of an array of mobile element with a common descent, the study of related fossils, and construction of a global database of mobile element associated genetic variation should prove useful for the identification of the geographic affiliation of unknown human DNA samples.

A3. Systems With Sex-Specific Transmission

a. Mitochondrial DNA (mtDNA)

Mitochondria are multiple organelles in the cytoplasm of the cell. Mitochondrial DNA (mtDNA) analysis has been demonstrated to be an effective technique for forensic identification in cases where the evidential material recovered is insufficient or inappropriate for chromosomal analysis.

Mitochondria are considered to be the "powerhouses of the cell" in that they are the primary means of oxidative respiration of the cell. That is, they are vital for utilization of oxygen to generate energy in the form of phosphorylated compounds. Thus, they provide energy that fuels the multiple reactions necessary for the body to function. They are found outside the nucleus in the cytoplasm of the cell.

Mitochondria contain their own DNA. This DNA differs from that found in the nucleus in several ways:

First, it is smaller than nuclear DNA, consisting of a single circular, double-stranded molecule that is 16,569 base pairs in length. The mtDNA genome provides an efficient coding entity in that it contains 37 genes, including 13 protein-coding genes, 2 ribosomal RNA (rRNA) genes, and 22 transfer RNA (tRNA) genes. Only a small region of the circular genome is noncoding. An *Mbo* I restriction site within the major noncoding region has been arbitrarily designated as the origin of the circular DNA, and the base pairs are numbered sequentially proceeding counterclockwise. In 1981, Anderson, et al. published the complete sequence of mtDNA from a composite of DNA from a human placenta and HeLa cells with ambiguous areas "filled in" with bovine mtDNA sequence. This sequence, commonly known as "the Anderson sequence" is the standard to which mtDNA sequence variations are compared. Polymorphisms are customarily indicated as differences from this reference sequence.

Second, mtDNA is inherited exclusively from the mother, whereas nuclear DNA (except for X and Y chromosomes) is inherited equally from both parents. This maternal inheritance is due to the fact that at conception all of the mitochondria come from the egg. Since mtDNA is passed directly from grandmother to mother to child it serves as an identity marker for maternal relatives. This clonal inheritance makes mtDNA useful in identity testing. For example, an inclusion or exclusion may be made, as with autosomal nuclear DNA, when the sample sequence is compared to that of a subject. However, using mitochondrial DNA, the same information can be obtained by testing the subject's sibling, mother, maternal grandmother, or maternal aunts or uncles.

Third, rather than carrying two different copies of DNA in equal number as observed with autosomal DNA markers, a single sequence of the mitochondrial DNA predominates. In other words, this is essentially a haploid sequence. (For exceptions to this, see heteroplasmy, below, in this section.) The designation of the dominant sequence is usually displayed as variations compared with the Anderson sequence standard. Sequence variation at individual sites are not independent. Each sequence variant, or haplotype, is considered as a single entity. Thus, discrimination power is determined essentially by comparing the sample sequence with a database of mtDNA sequences to identify its frequency in the population. This limits the power of discrimination of the mtDNA sequence to its relation to known databases. By contrast, autosomal markers display higher discrimination power because they provide independent markers whose power can be multiplied using the product rule (see II, 7b.).

Fourth, each mitochondrion has multiple copies of the circular-duplex 16,569-bp DNA. Each human cell contains several hundred to several thousand mitochondria; thus there are many more copies of mtDNA than nuclear DNA present in the cell, offering improved sensitivity in forensic analyses compared to nuclear DNA typing techniques. In some cases, nuclear DNA is significantly degraded, cannot be isolated, or is present in extremely limited amounts. Thus, mtDNA may provide results, when genomic DNA does not, allowing for the analysis of hair shafts, feathers, teeth, old bones, charred remains, and other biological specimens known to contain little or no useful nuclear DNA.

The amount of mtDNA isolated from forensic specimens may be very small, so DNA extraction is followed by PCR amplification. During the PCR process, specific hypervariable regions of the mtDNA genome are amplified with PCR primers designed to distinguish the mtDNA from the nuclear DNA. For individual identification purposes, attention is focused on DNA sequence analysis of a region that is greater than 1,000 bases in a portion of the mtDNA genome that is known as the "control region" or "displacement loop" (D-loop). The control region is the major noncoding segment of human mtDNA. It is instrumental in the regulation and initiation of synthesis of mtDNA gene products and replication of the heavy strand of the mtDNA. DNA sequencing of the complete control region demonstrates that variability is concentrated in two hypervariable (HV) segments of about 300 base pairs each, with the first segment (HV1) having more variability than the second segment (HV2).

Databases are being developed to exploit the full discrimination potential of the D-loop sequence as more laboratories submit sequences. Thus far, sequences from large

Caucasian populations have shown no mtDNA sequence occurring with a frequency of greater than 4 percent. Most haplotypes are found only once in a database. Some more frequent sequences have been found within some African tribal and Native American populations.

Although no comprehensive studies have been performed, evolutionary studies have estimated that the average fixed mutation rate for the mtDNA control region is one nucleotide difference per 300 generations, or one difference every 6,000 years. Consequently, one would not expect to observe many examples of nucleotide differences between maternal relatives.

Issues have been raised concerning the extent of heteroplasmy, or more than one mitochondrial genotype in a cell. Replicate hair samples have shown varying degrees of heteroplasmy, which is more common in hair than other tissues. For this reason, current policy concerning matches between known and questioned samples is that an exclusion cannot be made on the basis of one base pair difference between them.

Recently there have been reports of recombination in mitochondria (Awadalla et al. 1999). The evidence is indirect, based on evolutionary arguments. For contrasting views, see Macaulay et al. (1999) and Eyre-Walker et al. (1999). If recombination occurs, it is very rare and not likely to complicate forensic analysis. Mutation and heteroplasmy are far more significant factors.

Advantages:

1. Since there are multiple mitochondria per cell, and with the use of PCR methods, extremely small amounts of DNA material can be informative. Thus, some samples, not amenable to use with nuclear DNA markers, can be analyzed using mitochondrial DNA markers.

2. The small mtDNA molecule is not degraded as fast as nuclear DNA.

3. Because the transmission of mtDNA is from mother to all her children, this is a particularly useful marker in tracing family lineages.

4. Because most mitochondrial haplotypes are found only once in a database, the discriminating power is larger than a single nuclear locus.

Limitations:

1. Since all the descendants through the female line are identical, this cannot be used to distinguish among members of a sibship or maternal relatives.

2. Since there is very little, if any, recombination, the discrimination power of the system is limited by the size of the database.

3. Heteroplasmy (the occurrence of more than one mitochondrial type in a single cell or person) can complicate the analysis.

4. Because the entire mitochondrial genome is inherited as a unit, it is equivalent to a single nuclear locus. Hence, the discriminatory power is limited by the size of the database.

b. Y Chromosome Markers

Several genetic markers have been identified on the Y chromosome. The Y chromosome is a nuclear DNA present in one copy per cell and only in males. It displays paternal inheritance, that is, it is transmitted from the father to each son. There are two regions of the Y chromosome that are homologous with and exchange parts with the X chromosome; these are called pseudoautosomal regions. However, the regions used for forensic analysis do not undergo genetic recombination, so that the alleles at the various loci are permanently linked and form a *haplotype* (a specific combination of linked alleles at several loci). Given the lack of recombination, the Y chromosome loci are not independent and thus, the product rule cannot be used to estimate population frequencies at multiple loci. So the Y chromosome markers collectively are inherited as if they were one locus with a large number of alleles and the population frequency of a given haplotype is determined by counting in a population database.

Y chromosome markers consist of STR loci and SNPs as observed with other nuclear DNA markers. Several representatives of both marker types have been studied across a large number of different populations. Alleles of STR and SNP loci can be used interchangeably to provide haplotype information. At present, well over 100 loci are known, mostly SNPs, but there are several STRs.

Like mitochondrial DNA, Y chromosome haplotype markers also are valuable as lineage markers for reconstructing family relationships. In this case, sample material from a male individual may be compared with a subject or the subject's brother, father, paternal grandfather, or paternal uncles for identification purposes. Their effectiveness in lineage studies extends to questions of common ancestral geographic origin. The use of mitochondrial and Y chromosome markers complement one another in such analyses.

Y chromosome markers are useful in the analysis of semen stains. Eliminating the need to separate semen and vaginal epithelial cells prior to analysis, these markers reveal only the male contribution of mixed samples from rape case swabs. This is particularly useful in cases of multiple male contributors to such samples. Y markers also are useful for resolving mixed samples in which more than one male contributed to saliva or blood samples.

The Y chromosome displays much more variability between groups and less within than autosomal loci. Hence, it has greater use for identifying the geographical origin. It must be remembered, however, that the Y chromosome, because of its male-to-male transmission, often has a different evolutionary pattern. Hence, it may reflect only the ancestry of the Y chromosome and not that of most of the genome.

There is a striking difference between STRs and SNPs. STRs show small values of θ whereas SNPs show large values (Hammer, personal communication). The reason is probably the high mutation rate of STRs. But, whatever the explanation, the two kinds of markers can serve different purposes. SNPs are particularly useful for tracing group differences, where STRs are more useful for individual comparisons.

Advantages:

    1. Since the Y chromosome is transmitted intact to all male progeny, it is particularly useful in tracing family relationships among males.

2. Because of patrilineal transmission and the lack of recombination, Y chromosome markers can be used to measure relatedness of individuals with a common geographical origin.

Limitations:

1. Since there is no recombination among the loci, the discriminatory power of the system is limited by the size of the database.

A4. Separation, Detection, and Amplification of DNA

Following are several techniques that can be expected in the foreseeable future. Some are already in place. Undoubtedly, there will be developments in the next decade that are not foreseen now. We reiterate one point, however. The CODIS system of 13 STR loci involves a large investment of time and facilities in a large number of laboratories. We expect it to remain in place for at least the 10-year period that we are attempting to foresee. Those new developments most likely to find wide usage are those that can be fitted into the existing system. Several of those discussed below have this property.

We must remember that this analysis provides just a snapshot in time of a rapidly moving revolution. The next 2 years, 5 years, or 10 years of global progress in technology could make this analysis look very shortsighted indeed. In addition to technical progress, commercial, legal, and political forces will play a significant role in determining the future level of use of some of these technologies.

a. Gel Electrophoresis

Gel electrophoresis is a technique used to separate DNA fragments based on their length. Each DNA sample is composed of units, called nucleotides. Each nucleotide contains a sugar, a base, and a phosphate backbone. The phosphate backbone, which links the nucleotides together, creates a negative charge. When subjected to an electric field, DNA moves toward the positive pole. This process is called electrophoresis.

Gel electrophoresis is a common adaptation of this process, which includes electrophoresis of the DNA through a porous medium. The original medium was starch, but current media include agarose and polyacrylamide, which can be prepared as liquids and set into gelatinous solids before use. The rate of DNA migration through the pores depends on pore size of the medium and the voltage of the electrophoresis. While all DNA molecules are pulled toward the positive electrode, small molecules move more rapidly than larger ones, despite the same charge to mass ratio. Thus, the DNA molecules are separated into classes based on length. By comparison with standard DNAs of known length migrating under the same conditions, the nucleotide length of sample DNAs can easily be determined.

Agarose gel electrophoresis is generally used with VNTR loci (A1.a, p. 37) and Southern hybridization analysis (A4.b, p.51), while polyacrylamide gels are generally used with STRs (A1.b, p. 39) and pentanucleotide repeats (A1.c, p. 42). This is done because the agarose gels are more effective for separation of larger DNA molecules (100 to 10,000 bases generated by restriction analysis, while the polyacrylamide gels work well with smaller ones (50 to 500 bases) created by amplification. Replacement of the gel with a sieving medium in a small bore tube is referred to as capillary electrophoresis (A4.e, p.52).

b. Southern Hybridization

The Southern hybridization process is named after E.M. Southern, who developed and published the method in 1975. Digestion of a human genomic DNA sample with a restriction endonuclease generates a very large number of DNA fragments. Some are longer than others. Subjecting the mixture to gel electrophoresis (A4.a, p. 50) generates a gradation of fragments in the gel based on size, these classes being distinguished by their length. Even so, each class contains a complex mixture of DNA fragments.

To determine the presence or absence of a particular fragment, such as a specific allele of a VNTR locus, the separated DNA fragments from the sample are denatured, that is, separated into their two component strands, usually by treatment with alkali, and transferred to a thinner, more sold support, a membrane, usually made of cellulose or nylon. The membrane is exposed in a liquid solution to a probe, that is, a DNA sequence specific to the VNTR locus. The probe is also single stranded, and mixing it under appropriate conditions with the sample fragments allows hybridization between the sample DNA and probe DNA, to occur only at the sites of complementary sequences (that is, where the sample and probe sequences are the same except that where one has a T the other has an A, and so on, so they match perfectly by Watson-Crick pairing rules). Thus, labels that are attached to probes are also localized to the position(s) of the specific sample allele(s).

Probes generally contain either radioactive labels or an enzyme that can convert a substrate into a luminescent output. In either case, the generated energy can be captured on film to display the position of each allele. Sizes of the alleles can be compared with size standards to assist with this process.

c. Polymerase Chain Reaction (PCR)

In 1985 (see Mullis and Faloona 1987) a process was reported by which specific portions of the sample DNA can be amplified almost indefinitely (Saiki et al. 1985, 1988). This has revolutionized the whole field of DNA study. The process, the polymerase chain reaction (PCR), mimics the biological process of DNA replication, but confines it to specific DNA sequences of interest.

In this process, the DNA sample is denatured into the separate individual strands. Two DNA primers are used to hybridize to two corresponding nearby sites on opposite DNA strands in such a fashion that the normal enzymatic extension of the active terminal of each primer (that is, the 3' end) leads toward the other primer. In this fashion, two new copies of the sequence of interest are generated.

Repeated denaturation, hybridization, and extension in this fashion produce an exponentially growing number of copies of the DNA of interest. The denaturation is generally performed by heating, and in this case using, replication enzymes that are tolerant of high temperatures (Taq DNA polymerase). Instruments that perform thermal cycling are now readily available from commercial sources. This process can produce a million-fold or greater amplification of the desired region in 2 hours or less.

While the target is greatly amplified over its source in the sample, it is not homogeneous. Furthermore, two alleles from a single locus may have been amplified, but not separated, during the amplification process. For these reasons, the amplified DNA is separated to allow followup analysis. Gel electrophoresis (A4.a, p. 50), reverse dot blot (A4.d, p. 52), and capillary electrophoresis (A4.e) are three commonly employed methods to separate the amplified allele segments based either on their size or sequence.

For amplified STR loci, electrophoretic conditions (A4.a and A4.e) are used to separate the alleles into a linear array. For amplified SNPs (A2.a, p. 43), the reverse dot procedure (A4.d) and hybridization arrays (A4.e) can be used to separate amplified materials of interest. Alleles are then detected by colorimetric, silver stain, or fluorescent detection.

d.   Reverse Dot Blot

The reverse dot blot procedure is a detection method used primarily to identify SNPs (A2.a, A2.b, A2.c, pp. 43–45) in amplified DNA. DNA probes are affixed to a membrane. During amplification, a biotin label is incorporated into the amplified alleles. The amplified DNA is denatured and hybridized with the immobilized probes. Hybridization occurs only to the probes that match perfectly in DNA sequence. One immobilized probe located at one particular site on the membrane is used to detect each sequence variant.

Following hybridization of the denatured PCR product to the probe array, a streptavidin-enzyme conjugate is allowed to bind to the biotin-labeled PCR product that has hybridized to the immobilized probes. A chromogenic substrate is added and, in positions containing hybridized DNA sequences and a corresponding streptavidin-enzyme, the substrate is converted into a blue color that precipitates on the membrane, identifying the presence of a sequence match. Strips of membrane may contain multiple dots, each with the ability to analyze the present or absence of one base in a sequence. More recently, a line format has been used in place of the dots.

e.   Capillary Electrophoresis (CE)

Capillary electrophoresis (CE) and slab gel electrophoresis are standard techniques for the separation and analysis of DNA fragments. For DNA applications, CE refers to an electrophoretic separation within a small diameter capillary (a long tube made of fused silica, typically 50 μ internal diameter) that is filled with a sieving medium. The sieving medium is typically an entangled polymer that is designed to separate DNA fragments on the basis of size. Compared to slab gel electrophoresis, CE offers the advantages of faster analysis times for small numbers of samples and increased automation.

Currently, the CE systems that are commonly used for the analysis of STRs utilize one capillary and can automatically analyze one sample every 30 minutes. Multiplex PCR and the use of several different fluorescent dye labels enables the simultaneous analysis of 10 or more STR loci. The multiplex/multicolor PCR products for each sample are combined with an internal size standard (DNA fragments of known size labeled with a different dye color), heat denatured, then placed in a 96-well tray on the CE instrument. An autosampler robot on the CE instrument presents each sample to the capillary for automated electrokinetic injection. Electrophoresis through the sieving medium in the capillary separates the DNA fragments by size. A laser continuously illuminates a detection window that is located near the end of the capillary. The fluorescently tagged DNA molecules are detected during electrophoresis as they reach this laser detection window (smaller DNA molecules reach the window before larger molecules). The laser-induced fluorescence is continuously monitored and detected on a CCD (charge coupled device) camera, which simultaneously detects and distinguishes the different fluorescent dye colors. The capillary is then automatically replenished with fresh sieving medium to prepare for the next sample. A tray of 96 samples can be sequentially analyzed by the instrument without the need for user intervention.

The collected data are analyzed by software which automatically determines allele sizes based on a standard curve, as defined by the known sizes and measured detection times for the internal size standard fragments. Genotypes are determined by comparison of sample allele sizes to the sizes observed for allelic ladder alleles in a different injection; this genotyping process is automated using available data analysis software.

These same CE systems are also capable of automated fluorescence DNA sequencing. In particular, it is expected that mitochondrial DNA sequencing by CE will become a standard method. The electrophoresis time for sequencing samples is typically 1 to 2 hours.

Continuous advancements in CE will offer higher throughput, greater automation, and faster analysis times. Recently, multiple capillary instruments have become available that simultaneously analyze 8 samples and 96 can be analyzed eventually without human intervention. Another recent advancement is the ability to analyze five dye colors (versus four in earlier generations); this expansion in dye detection will result in an increase in the number of STR loci that can be simultaneously analyzed for each sample.

Greater automation will be achieved as data analysis software improves toward minimizing the time required by a human operator to examine the data that are collected from the CE systems. Computer databases also will integrate with the CE instruments to further automate the scheduling and management of samples in the laboratory.

Finally, faster analysis times will be achieved as the CE dimensions become smaller. Smaller capillary dimensions allow for the use of higher voltages, and thus faster electrophoresis times. Smaller dimensions may also pave the way toward integration of the different DNA analysis processes (sample prep, PCR, CE) on a single device. Devices that are sufficiently small may be transportable such that analysis could take place outside of a standard laboratory.

For recent reviews, see Butler (1998), Righetti and Gelfi (1998), and Thormann et al. (1999).

f.   Miniaturization and Chip Technologies

Advanced primarily by a small number of academic and industrial laboratories, and aided by Federal funding, new methods that combine computer technologies and biotechnologies are rapidly appearing. These approaches show outstanding promise to revolutionize once again the speed, safety, and efficiency with which genetic analyses, including forensic DNA identification, can be performed. While still in development, their application in this field is expected to be widespread in 5 to 10 years. The cost for these advances is not yet known, but as with many new technologies, it is expected to decrease dramatically with expanded use.

The leading approaches employ photolithography and chemical etching techniques similar to those used in the manufacture of microelectronic chips. Hybridization arrays also can be made by spotting. However, the microchannels etched into these chips are used to transport sample materials such as blood or purified DNA. In addition, transport of liquid reagents, like those used to carry out many of the manipulations central to traditional DNA analysis, allow these tasks to be performed on a miniaturized scale.

Typical dimensions for microchannels are 10 microns deep and 10 to 100 microns wide. The support material can be glass, silicon, quartz, or plastic. Rather than employing pumps present in larger instrumentation, fluid movement is accomplished by electrokinetic forces induced by application of small voltages to specific regions of the chip. This approach provides a more precise measurement and greater reproducibility to the movement of liquids. Standard biological procedures such as pipetting, mixing, and separation can be mimicked by this approach.

More complex formulation of these techniques produces miniaturized versions of commonly used biological methods such as sample preparation, the polymerase chain reaction, capillary electrophoresis, and STR fragment detection and analysis. The "hardwiring" of the chip design determines the nature of the analytical steps to be performed, and the software or programming allows variation of the mixing and separation techniques.

Several potential advantages of this approach are readily apparent. With miniaturization of the process, less time is required to heat, cool, or transport sample and reagent materials. In fact, model systems suggest that the entire PCR and capillary electrophoretic separation of resulting STR products can be accomplished in a few minutes rather than several hours as required with currently employed methods.

An additional advantage is the use of less reagent materials in the processing. While this has an obvious benefit in lowering cost, it sometimes has the added benefit of safety in the handling of less of these sometimes toxic materials and in simplifying disposal needs. Once these types of systems are fully developed, the operations will occur largely without the need of human intervention, which will mean that individuals who formerly performed these techniques are freed for higher level functions.

The approaches just described offer an efficient transition from current technologies and methods while maintaining the value of predetermined profiles using the 13 STR core loci. However, they are not the only chip technologies being advanced. A variety of techniques include the use of solid surfaces to retain large arrays of different DNA sequences that can be used in a variety of creative ways.

Such hybridization arrays are exemplified by the use of oligonucleotides (short synthetically created DNA sequences) which hybridize (that is, specifically capture by interaction with complementary DNA sequence) short segments of DNA from a human DNA sample. Manipulation of these captured segments has allowed determination of single nucleotide polymorphisms (SNPs, A2.a, p. 43), of STR repeat number content (for example, using a technique that employs electric fields to optimize the hybridization process), and of the DNA sequence analysis of extended segments of DNA being analyzed.

This latter group of techniques offers the possibility of testing many DNA sites in the genome simultaneously, perhaps even thousands of sites. Thus, these approaches will provide an enormous ability to discriminate individuals in the population. In addition, key reagents required for these approaches are built into the chip itself, requiring only the addition of sample material.

In comparing the miniaturization processes described first, above, to the hybridization array technologies just mentioned, the miniaturization processes offer the advantage of complete compatibility with the existing CODIS database structure based upon the use of STR loci as genetic markers. Any new variant alleles appearing in the CODIS core loci will be readily detected and interpreted in much the same fashion as observed with current methods. Thus, today's data entries and future ones may be seamlessly compared.

In the system mentioned earlier (II, 8.a, p. 28), eight STR loci (CSF1PO, TPOX, TH01, vWA, D16S539, D7S820, D13S317 and D5S818) could be analyzed to 4-base resolution in 2 minutes. The partial repeat of TH01, allele 9.3, could be detected in 10 minutes (Schmalzing et al. 1999). Such fast, miniaturized systems should be available for routine use in a few years, surely in the 10 years of our purview. Systems such as this, that improve the handling of the existing 13 loci, should be the first to come into use, since they fit in with the widespread use of these loci.

On the other hand, the use of the hybridization array technologies requires the knowledge of the sequence of all alleles prior to preparation of the hard-wired chip. Thus, new variants will be less confidently detected or interpreted. In addition, while the use of hybridization arrays in combination with electronic hybridization techniques has demonstrated success with a model STR system, adaptation to all the CODIS STR core loci may prove difficult. Since the STR core loci are expected to be used for an extended lifetime of at least 10 years in the national and international database systems, we expect that hybridization array technologies will find forensic use primarily in other applications employing SNPs and sequence analysis in mitochondrial DNA analysis, Y chromosome genetics, population group identification, and confirmatory analysis of samples identified by a database search.

g. Mass Spectrometry

Since its development in the late 1980s, matrix-assisted laser desorption mass spectrometry (MALDI-MS) has become a very powerful tool for addressing analytical questions in chemistry, biology, and forensics. In contrast to laser desorption/ionization (LDI) the analyzed molecules are embedded in a crystalline matrix of small organic compounds, which have a key function in this technique. While LDI allows a detection of molecules up to 2000 daltons, analytic ions with masses of several hundred thousand daltons, such as small STR DNA fragments, can be investigated by MALDI-MS.

MALDI-MS technology consists of a series of steps to accurately measure DNA molecules. First, small quantities of PCR-amplified DNA products are generated and placed on a substrate surface, usually in an arrayed configuration. Second, the small products are prepared for analysis by co-crystallization with the proper organic matrix. Third, the products are accurately measured. This is accomplished by allowing the matrix molecules to absorb a brief pulse of laser irradiation leading to a spontaneous volatilization and ionization of matrix and DNA fragments. These gas-phase ions thus become amenable to mass spectrometric analysis. The determination of the molecular weight of the molecule is achieved by the measurement of the time-of-flight (TOF) of the ions which is proportional to its mass in the mass spectrometer. This process is known as matrix-assisted laser desorption /ionization time-of-flight mass spectrometry (MALDI-TOF-MS).

The use of MALDI-TOF-MS allows the user to achieve rapid results, performing STR typing at a rate of a few seconds per sample, including computerized analysis. The resulting mass sizes of the DNA fragments are very accurate and typing can be achieved without the need for allelic ladders. DNA is measured directly and no fluorescent or radioactive labels are required. To eliminate hand manipulation that can result in imprecision, samples are usually prepared by use of a robotic system and data collection is automated. Thus, the technology provides a high-throughput system capable of processing thousands of samples per day.

Despite all the above advantages, there are a few problems with the technology that must be considered. Mass spectrometry sensitivity and resolution are diminished when either the DNA fragment size or the salt content of the sample is too high. Research must be done to redesign PCR primers that will bind close to the repeat region and thus enhance resolution and sensitivity of the PCR products by reducing the STR allele sizes. Microdialysis is employed to help reduce the salt content of the sample.

MALDI-TOF-MS provides an alternative technology for mass typing of samples, allowing rapid database entry for CODIS implementation. Several organizations have focused efforts to achieve this possibility. Whether MALDI-TOF-MS technology gains widespread acceptance or not depends upon commitments made by commercial or research organizations to provide significant cost advantages over current means of evaluating STR markers, given that high throughput will be a major benefit.

A5. **Statistics and Population Genetics**

Here we develop more fully some of the concepts that were presented in section II, 7 and summarize the various formulae used so they will be in one place.

A5.1. **Technical Considerations**

a. *Population Structure*

The traditional measures of population structure were developed by Wright (see 1951). Wright measured the effect of subdivision on homozygosity by F_{IT} and on the probability of identical alleles in different individuals of the same subgroup by F_{ST}. Equations (1) from section II, 7, p. 22 are modified to read:

For homozygotes: $P(A_iA_i) = p_i2 + p_i(1-p_i)F_{IT}$ (A1a)

For heterozygotes: $P(A_iA_j) = 2p_ip_j(1- F_{IT})$ (A1b)

With random mating within the subgroups, F_{IT} and F_{ST} become the same and we shall designate this by θ. The designation θ comes from Cockerham (1969), who developed a similar system.

As an example, recent analyses of STRs (Chakraborty 2000 personal communication and Budowle et al. 2000) show the following values for θ in different populations:

Population	Chakraborty	Budowle
African	0.0018	0.0006
Caucasian	0.0022	-0.0005
Asian	0.0050	0.0039
Hispanic		0.0021
Native American	0.0347	0.0282

The smaller values of Budowle are the result of his sample being restricted to the United States, whereas the Chakraborty data are worldwide. The NRC report (NRC 1996) recommended for general usage with VNTRs a conservative value of 0.01, and data such as the above show that this is reasonable for STRs as well.

In Native Americans, in contrast, the tribal structure is reflected in much higher values of θ. Clearly, frequencies for particular tribes are needed, or a larger value of θ (e.g., 0.03) must be employed. NRC (1996) recommended other procedures for dealing with tribes in which relevant data are missing.

b. The Sib Method

Instead of calculating the conditional probability that a random sample of DNA matches the evidence sample, we calculate the probability of a specific match for a (possibly hypothetical) sibling of the person contributing the evidence sample. Then we can be confident that the probability would be smaller for any less related individual, including other relatives or a person chosen from the same small group. So this provides a "safe" (i.e., conservative) estimate. It also has other salutary attributes.

The approximate conditional match probabilities for sibs are:

Homozygotes: $P(A_iA_i|A_iA_i) = (1 + 2p_i + p_i^2 + 4\theta)/4$ (A2a)

Heterozygotes: $P(A_iA_j|A_iA_j) = (1 + p_i + p_j + 2p_ip_j + 2\theta)/4$ (A2b)

Here are the population match probabilities for random pairs of siblings in four population groups, (assuming $\theta = 0$) for the 13 core STR loci and for a larger group of 21 loci (data on additional loci from J. Schumm, 1999 personal communication).

Group	Afr. Amer.	Cauc. Amer.	Asian Amer.	Hispan. Amer.
13 core loci	2.6×10^{-6}	3.1×10^{-6}	2.1×10^{-6}	3.7×10^{-6}
21 loci	7.4×10^{-10}	1.5×10^{-9}	2.5×10^{-9}	2.5×10^{-9}

Two things stand out: (1) The match probabilities are quite small, even when only the 13 core loci are used, and become smaller with more loci. The technical power is now available to avoid most of the uncertainties caused by ignorance of the population substructure and the possibility of near relatives in the population. (2) The differences among population groups is small. For 13 loci, the largest is less than two times the value of the smallest. The reason for the fairly close agreement among groups is that so much of the probability is determined by the factor 1/4, which is constant for all population groups.

There is always some uncertainty about whether the HW and linkage equilibrium assumptions are appropriate. For sibs, this uncertainty is greatly reduced, again because of the factor 1/4, which does not depend on allele frequencies. This factor depends only on Mendelian segregation and is not affected by allele frequencies or population structure. Likewise, the value of θ does not depend on allele frequencies. Furthermore, linkage disequilibrium is not an issue for the factor 1/4, since unlinked loci behave independently in the parents. So any effects of homozygosity within loci and nonrandomness between loci are largely diluted out, especially when the number of alleles at each locus is large and no one allele has a high frequency.

Is such a procedure likely to be used in the future? It would presumably be welcomed by those who are most concerned with the validity of the assumptions about population structure or about the possibility of undetected relatives. It would also be welcomed by those who dislike putting people into groups. But it might require more loci and therefore increase expense. In the future, the number of loci is likely to be large enough and costs low enough that this calculation could be applied routinely. Meanwhile, the 13 core loci are adequate for most situations and when match probabilities are already very low additional loci may not increase confidence.

c. Individualization

The FBI uses the following principle: If the probability is substantially less than the reciprocal of the United States population, then "to a reasonable degree of scientific certainty" the profile is defined as unique in the United States. The FBI procedure assumes random mating proportions and independence of the allele frequencies at different loci, or uses $\theta = 0.01$ (or 0.03 for Native Americans). Then, if P is the calculated profile frequency, the probability of not finding it in a population of N randomly chosen individuals is $(1-P)^N$, so the probability of finding it at least once is $1 - (1 - P)^N$. To hedge against uncertainties of assumptions and numbers, the FBI introduced several conservative modifications. First, they ask that this probability be less than $\alpha = 0.01$. Second, they chose P as the largest value among the four common group databases. Third, they multiply P by 10, to allow for uncertainties in the assumptions, based on empirical data from FBI (1993) presented in NRC (1996). Using 260 million as the United States population, N, this leads to the statement that if P, modified as above, is less than 3.9×10^{-11}, the suspect DNA and the evidence DNA came from the same person "to a reasonable degree of scientific certainty" (Budowle et al. 2000). Using the product rule, the probability that two randomly chosen Caucasian Americans will have the same 13-locus STR profile is 1.7×10^{-15} (table A2, p. 41) so a 13-locus match would often meet the criterion for individualization.

The FBI procedure (DAB 2000) includes allowances for population structure, including Equations 2 (p. 24) when it is assumed that the contributor and accused are from the same subgroup. θ is taken as 0.01. Similar procedures are given for those populations, such as Native Americans, not included in the large databases; this means taking $\theta = 0.03$ and smaller N. As for relatives, the FBI says: "In certain cases, it may be necessary to consider the probability that a relative of a suspect may have the same profile." In these cases formulae for the appropriate relatives are given (NRC 1996, p. 113; Budowle et al. 2000, p. 68; Equations A6 and A7, p. 64).

d. Database Search

Recently, there has been more emphasis in the statistical literature on the likelihood ratio approach. Those who advocate this approach are critical of the recommendations of both NRC recommendations (e.g., Evett and Weir 1998, pp. 219–222). They point out that the likelihood ratio contains all the evidence in the data (Royall 1997; Donnelly and Friedman 1999), and that manner of ascertainment is irrelevant to the likelihood ratio. They take the finding of a match in the database as given, not as a possible future event. For example, assume that there has been a database search and one match was found. Then, employing conditional probabilities, one can write the likelihood ratio for the probability of finding one match and N-1 nonmatches under the hypotheses that the source of the evidence DNA was in the database and the alternative hypothesis that he was not. Evett and Weir, following Balding and Donnelly (1996), find that the database search makes very little difference to the likelihood ratio, and that what difference it does make is such as to reduce rather than increase the match probability.

We noted in section II, 7 that a likelihood ratio can be converted into a probability by the use of prior odds. The prior odds depend on the strength of non-DNA information in the case. In a database search the prior odds of a particular profile being included depends, among other things, on the size and randomness of the database. If the search was of DNA profiles from convicted felons, the prior odds are affected by the recidivism rate. On the other hand, if the database is a random sample of the entire population, the prior odds that a random individual is the culprit is small. Another instance in which the likelihood ratio is the same, but the prior odds are quite different, is the case of a sample from a victim. So far, the courts have been reluctant to accept prior odds, and their future acceptability remains to be seen.[15]

A database of convicted felons and a database that approximates a random sample of the population are quite different. Recidivism rates for many offenses are known to be high, much higher than would be expected from the rate of new offenses in the population (Greenfeld, 1997). Thus, the prior probability of guilt for a person obtained from a database of convicted felons may then be comparable to that for a suspect identified by eyewitness or detective work. There is therefore justification for the common practice of using the likelihood ratio by itself as evidence, since this is likely to overwhelm any difference in prior odds. With likelihood ratios of 10^{12} and often much greater, prior odds of, say, 0.1, are swamped out.

If in the future databases that approximate a random sample from the population become common, then identification of a suspect from such a database runs a risk of a random

---

15. Stockmarr (1999) has argued that the proper likelihood ratio in the single match case is 1/Np, agreeing numerically to the NRC (1996) recommendation. He has recognized that the manner in which the person is identified should be taken into account. The statistics literature, however, shows a preference to follow the principle given above that the effect of the database search should be incorporated into the prior odds, not the likelihood ratio. If the prior probability is the reciprocal of the database size, the result is the same as the NRC (1996) recommendation.

profile match, and the risk increases with the size of the database. Looking to the future, if such databases become widely used, one possibility is to follow the recommendation of NRC (1992) and adopt the procedure of calculating the specific match probability for loci not used in identification of the subject (Morton 1997). In other words, the database match is investigatory, not conclusionary. Alternatively, the DAB (2000) recommends following NRC (1996) and multiplying the match probability by the size of the database searched. Or, if a likelihood ratio approach is favored, the prior odds can be set at an appropriately low value.

e. Inferring Group or Traits From a DNA Sample

Recently, there has been increasing discussion and study of the possibility of using a DNA sample to determine characteristics of the person who left the sample. One possibility is to use the frequencies in the different databases to infer the population to which the person leaving the DNA belongs. If a crime-scene sample were more likely to have come from a Caucasian American than from an African American, this information would be useful in the search for the culprit. It would be similar to an eyewitness account, where the witness had only a fleeting glimpse that indicated the probable group of the culprit but provided no specific traits.

The possibility of identifying the biological ancestry of the person contributing a DNA sample was discussed by Evett et al. (1992), employing a likelihood ratio criterion. Brenner (1997), studied a five-locus VNTR profile of an unknown serial rapist. Using a simple calculation using binned data, he found a likelihood ratio of 45 for a Caucasian American versus an African American, that is, the probability of this profile is 45 times as great if it came from a Caucasian American. This was consistent with what the police had suspected.

How typical is this result? We can calculate the geometric mean likelihood ratio when the 13 CORE STR loci are used. Formulae are given by Shriver et al. (1997) and in a form much simpler to compute by Brenner (1998). This formula yields a likelihood ratio of 43.5 for comparison of Caucasian Americans with African Americans. That is, if a random profile is chosen from a population its probability is about 45 times as great with the correct database as with the wrong one.

The likelihood ratio alone may be misleading. Finding a DNA profile that favors one group will have quite a different significance in a population where this group predominates, as opposed to one in which the group is rare. Suppose a DNA profile is 45 times as likely if it came from the African American population as if it came from the Caucasian American population. In the local community the ratio of African to Caucasian is 1:4. The posterior odds in favor of the evidence coming from a black person are reduced to (1/4)(45), or about 11.

So far, we have discussed what can be done using existing forensic databases. For the future, we can expect to find an increasing number of alleles at other loci that are associated with different groups. But we emphasize two things: (1) These are not the loci that are currently used in criminal investigation, so such identification could not be made without using different methods (in particular, STRs used for forensics do not include any such loci), and (2) any group identification is probabilistic, not certain.

One allele of the Duffy blood group is found in almost 100 percent of persons from parts of West Africa and is very rare in non-African populations. The reason is that this allele

(Duffy null) confers resistance to vivax malaria and has become fixed (or nearly so) in this part of the world where malaria is rampant.

The population distribution of Y chromosome sites differs greatly from that for autosomal loci. For STRs, about 95 percent of the population diversity is between individuals within major groups and less than 5 percent is between group means. For the Y chromosome, in contrast, about 53 percent is between groups. Thus, as more Y chromosome SNPs and STRs are available for study, the Y chromosome will be an increasingly effective way to judge a person's ancestry. For example, Native Americans have a specific Y haplotype that is very rare in other populations.

It is important to note that such designations reveal only an ancestral contribution. Finding a Duffy-null allele in a DNA sample means that the person is likely to have some African ancestry, whereas finding another Duffy allele means that there may be some non-African ancestry. One needs to be especially careful about the Y chromosome, in which the father to son transmission and sex-differences in migration patterns can lead to large differences between the Y and the other chromosomes. Thus, inferring external appearance (e.g., skin color) from analysis of a single locus, and especially the Y chromosome, may be grossly misleading.

The question of specific traits is different. As already emphasized, the loci now used for forensic identification and likely to be used in the future are not individually indicative of any external appearance. But a search for markers associated with specific traits will ultimately reveal them. Some laboratories are actively searching for such marker genes. For example, determining that a DNA sample was left by a person with red hair, dark skin pigment, straight hair, baldness, or color blindness may be practical soon, if not already. The number of common traits that are caused by single gene differences is not likely to be high, and using multifactorial phenotypes will be difficult, but may ultimately be useful. Yet, the Human Genome Project and other research efforts can be expected eventually to identify a number of genes leading to identifiable traits, especially rare ones. But this involves research in a direction quite different from that now employed in forensic work, in which the emphasis is on finding marker alleles not associated with identifiable traits.

Identical twins. If multiple markers can distinguish between any two individuals, including close relatives, there remains one class of relatives that will not be distinguished, namely identical twins. Since they began as a single fertilized egg, their DNA profiles are identical, except for possible somatic mutations. This suggests that looking at somatically mutable loci might be fruitful. The immunoglobulin genes are one possibility. Another possibility for future research is virus infections, especially those that are incorporated into the DNA. The insertion sites of retrovirus might be different in twins. Although such possibilities are impractical at present, they may not remain so. If more loci are used in the future, there may be instances in which identical twins differ in somatic mutations of STRs, or perhaps mtDNA, detectable from a blood stain. Of course twins may be distinguished by non-DNA means, such as fingerprints, when such evidence is available.

Recently, gene expression arrays for analyzing mRNA have become popular for genetic research. These devices permit thousands of genes to be assessed on a handheld chip, or on probes affixed to minute beads. These devices make it possible to determine the differences in gene expression (production of mRNA) between different samples. For example, genes are expressed at characteristic times in the life-cycle. Thus, old and young mice of the same inbred strain are easily distinguished. It is likely that, because of their different experiences, identical twins may express genes differentially at some loci and that this may form a basis for distinguishing between them.

Even though we cannot at this time be more specific, the pace of research in molecular genetics is such that we can look forward to a future time when even identical twins can be distinguished.

A5.2 Summary of Formulae

Here we summarize the formulae used in the report and provide further details and explanations. Most of these are available in NRC (1996) and, in greater detail and generality, in Evett and Weir (1998).

a. General Formulae

The average heterozygosity at a locus provides a simple index of the discriminatory power of the locus—the more heterozygous, the more discriminating. For comparing systems, the random mating (HW) assumption is usually used. For forensic calculations, modifications that take population structure into account are often preferred, as noted below.

The population homozygosity at a specific locus is given by

$$\text{hom} = \Sigma \, p_i^2 \qquad\qquad\qquad\qquad \text{(A1a)}$$

where p_i is the frequency of the ith allele and the sum is over all allele frequencies. The heterozygosity is the complement of the homozygosity, given by

$$\text{het} = 1 - \text{hom.} \qquad\qquad\qquad\qquad \text{(A1b)}$$

The discriminating power is more precisely estimated, however, by the probability of a match between two randomly chosen individuals. This is

$$\text{Population Match Prob.} = \Sigma_i (p_i^2)^2 + \Sigma_{i<j} (2p_i p_j)^2$$

$$= 2(\Sigma_i \, p_i^2)^2 - \Sigma_i \, p_i^4 \, . \qquad\qquad \text{(A2)}$$

where p_i and p_j are the frequencies of two different alleles. The second formula is much easier to calculate, since for n alleles it is necessary to sum over only n terms, rather than n(n+1)/2, the number of genotypes. For a system of multiple independent loci, the probabilities for the individual loci are multiplied.

The formulae above are used to compare the forensic value of different systems. For comparison purposes it is customary to ignore population structure. The formulae below, used for forensic calculations, take population structure into account.

Population structure. The genotype frequencies in a structured population, as stated earlier, are

$$A_i A_i: P_{ii} = p_i^2 + p_i(1-p_i)F_{IT} \qquad\qquad \text{(A3a)}$$

$$A_i A_j: P_{ij} = 2p_i p_j (1 - F_{IT}) \, , \, i \neq j \, . \qquad\qquad \text{(A3b)}$$

When there is random mating within each subpopulation, then F_{IT} can be replaced by F_{ST} or θ. θ can be defined by

$$\theta = \frac{f_S - f_T}{1 - f_T} \qquad . \qquad\qquad\qquad \text{(A4)}$$

In this formula f_S is the average probability that two alleles drawn randomly from the same subpopulation are the same allele; f_T is the probability of their being the same if they are drawn randomly from the total population. θ is thus a measure of population substructure, and for our purposes, assuming random mating in the subpopulations, its meaning is the same as Wright's F_{ST} and Nei's G_{ST}. We might add, however, that although equation (A4) provides an intuitively appealing definition, this is not the best way to calculate θ from actual data. For more appropriate procedures, see Weir (1996), pp. 161–190. For those who read the evolution literature, we note that θ as used here is not the same as θ used in molecular evolution to assess the effect of a finite population on random gene-frequency drift.

Conditional match probability corrected for population structure. It is possible, however, that the two persons come from the same subpopulation. In that situation, the conditional match probabilities in a structured population, as given by Equations 2 in section II, 7, p. 24, are approximately

$$P(A_iA_i|A_iA_i) \approx \frac{[2\theta + (1-\theta)p_i][3\theta + (1-\theta)p_i]}{(1 + \theta)(1 + 2\theta)} \qquad \text{(A5a)}$$

$$P(A_iA_j|A_iA_j) \approx \frac{2[\theta + (1-\theta)p_i][\theta + (1-\theta)p_j]}{(1 + \theta)(1 + 2\theta)} \qquad \text{(A5b)}$$

The recommendation in NRC (1996) was to use Equations A5 when the source of the evidence and the suspect are thought to be from the same subpopulation. However, others have advocated using this formula more generally since it is expected that the two persons may well belong to the same subpopulation, even if we do not know it (Evett and Weir, 1998).

To get an idea of the numerical effect of using Equations A5, instead of the simple Hardy-Weinberg assumption, we give some simple calculations. We assumed, for convenience, equal frequencies of all alleles and computed the effect of the two equations as a function of allele number. Assuming $\theta = 0.01$ and homozygotes in expected proportions, we have, for 13 loci:

Number of alleles	Population match probability Using HW	Using A5	Ratio
4	3.21×10^{-13}	5.85×10^{-13}	1.83
5	1.40×10^{-15}	3.26×10^{-15}	2.33
7	3.33×10^{-19}	1.26×10^{-18}	3.80
10	4.21×10^{-23}	3.27×10^{-22}	7.78

Clearly, the ratio increases as the number of alleles increases. It becomes large only when the probability is so small that a factor 10 discrepancy would not change the conclusion. We conclude that, although it may well be desirable to use Equations A5, it is not likely to change the conclusion.

As expected, increasing the value of θ increases the discrepancy between the two formulae. For example, with 5 alleles and $\theta = 0.03$, the ratio becomes 11.3 instead of 2.33. However, even a factor of 11 will be swamped by a probability of 10^{-15}.

Relatives. The conditional match probability for most relatives of degree F in a randomly mating, nonsubdivided population is

For homozygotes: A_iA_i: $p_i^2 + 4p_i(1 - p_i)F$ (A6a)

For heterozygotes: A_iA_j: $2p_ip_j + 2(p_i + p_j - 4p_ip_j)F$ (A6b)

where F is the kinship coefficient. Values for relatives of interest for forensics are $F = 1/4$ for parent and child, 1/8 for half sibs, 1/8 for uncle and nephew, and 1/16 for first cousins. Full siblings require a different formula, discussed below.

The kinship coefficient, F, of two individuals is the probability that two alleles, one from each individual, are identical by descent (both descended from the same allele in an ancestor, or one descended from the other). The inbreeding coefficient, also designated by F, of an individual is obviously the same as the kinship coefficient of its parents. Any confusion is avoided by single or double subscripts. The inbreeding coefficient of individual i is F_i. The kinship coefficient of two individuals j and k is F_{jk}. If j and k are parents of i, $F_i = F_{jk}$.

There is a simple algorithm for computing inbreeding and kinship coefficients, available in many textbooks (e.g., Hartl and Clark 1997; Crow and Kimura 1970, pp. 69–73; Cavalli-Sforza and Bodmer 1971).

Siblings. If the case requires match probabilities for full siblings, the approximate conditional match probabilities are

For homozygotes: A_iA_i: $(1 + 2p_i + p_i^2 + 4\theta)/4$ (A7a)

For heterozygotes: A_iA_j: $(1 + p_i + p_j + 2p_ip_j + 2\theta)/4$ (A7b)

where θ is the kinship coefficient of the population from which the parents are drawn. Note, as mentioned earlier, that there is always a factor 1/4 for sibs, regardless of the rarity of the alleles. The smaller p_i and p_j are, the more the 1/4 dominates. Since siblings necessarily come from the same subpopulation, the θ correction is in order. If $\theta < 0.01$, as most studies show, then the correction makes only a small difference. These formulae are approximations, although very good for multiallelic loci, since p_i, p_j, and θ are usually much less than 1; for exact formulae, see Weir (1994).

Population match probabilities for siblings. The match probability for two randomly chosen siblings is

Population match prob. $= (1 + 2\sum_i p_i^2 + 2(\sum_i p_i^2)^2 - \sum_i p_i^4)/4$ (A8)

where h is the homozygosity. Equation A8 is useful for comparison of different systems. For this purpose, we have omitted any θ correction.

b. Partial Matches

Increasingly with database searches, there are partial matches (that is, matches for several alleles, but not all). These may indicate that the two samples came from relatives. The example below shows the similarity between siblings.

There are often patterns that are clear from direct inspection. Siblings usually share both alleles at some loci, something that is rare for other relatives (unless the alleles are common). Parent and child always share one allele, but rarely two and never zero. Other less closely related pairs often share a single allele, but rarely two.

Although such inspection is often revealing, a more quantitative procedure is to compute the probability of observing the pedigree for different specified relationships, and compare these with unrelated persons or with other relatives. This can be done using k-coefficients. This approach traces back the pioneering work of Cotterman (1940).

Let k_2, $2k_1$, and k_0 be the probabilities that the two noninbred relatives have identical alleles at both loci, at one, or at none. Then the conditional match probabilities, making no allowance for population subdivision, are:

Relatives' genotypes		Frequency of the pair
1st	2nd	
A_iA_i	A_iA_i	$p_i^2[k_2 + 2k_1p_i + k_0p_i2]$
A_iA_i	A_iA_j	$p_i2[2k_1p_j + 2k_0p_ip_j]$
A_iA_i	A_jA_j	$p_i2[k_0p_j^2]$
A_iA_i	A_jA_k	$p_i^2[k_02p_jp_k]$
A_iA_j	A_iA_j	$2p_ip_j[k_2 + k_1p_i + k_1p_j + 2k_0p_ip_j]$
A_iA_j	A_iA_k	$2p_ip_j[k_1p_k + 2k_0p_ip_k]$
A_iA_j	A_kA_l	$2p_ip_j[k_02p_kp_l]$

The probabilities are given for ordered pairs. For example, with sibs the first relative may be the older sib and the second the younger. For unordered pairs the frequencies of all nonidentical pairs should be doubled.

Here is an instance in which the two samples shared two alleles at six loci, one at six, and none at one.

Locus	Genotypes Sample 1	Sample 2	Probability of these genotypes
D3S1358	17/16	17/16	$2p_{17}p_{16}(k_2 + k_1p_{16} + k_1p_{17} + 2k_0p_{17}p_{16})$
D7S820	12/8	12/8	$2p_{12}p_8(k_2 + k_1p_8 + k_1p_{12} + 2k_0p_{12}p_8)$
D16S539	14/8	14/8	$2p_{14}p_8(k_2 + k_1p_8 + k_1p_{14} + 2k_0p_{14}p_8)$
D21S11	33/30	33/30	$2p_{33}p_{30}(k_2 + k_1p_{30} + k_1p_{33} + 2k_0p_{33}p_{30})$
FGA	23/22	23/22	$2p_{23}p_{22}(k_2 + k_1p_{22} + k_1p_{23} + 2k_0p_{23}p_{22})$
TPOX	10/8	10/8	$2p_{10}p_8(k_2 + k_1p_8 + k_1p_{10} + 2k_0p_{10}p_8)$
THO1	6/6	9/9	$p_6{}^2k_0p_9{}^2$
CSF1PO	11/10	12/11	$2p_{11}p_{10}(k_1p_{12} + 2k_0p_{11}p_{12})$
D8S1179	12/8	13/12	$2p_{12}p_8(k_1p_{13} + 2k_0p_{13}p_{12})$
D13S317	9/8	12/9	$2p_9p_8(k_1p_{12} + 2k_0p_{12}p_9)$
D18S51	14/13	17/13	$2p_{14}p_{13}(k_1p_{17} + 2k_0p_{17}p_{13})$
vWA	19/17	17/15	$2p_{19}p_{17}(k_1p_{15} + 2k_0p_{17}p_{15})$
D5S818	12/12	12/11	$p_{12}{}^2(k_1p_{11} + 2k_0p_{12}p_{11})$

This sibship is rather unusual, but was chosen to highlight a particular feature of siblings, namely a substantial fraction of loci in which both alleles are shared.

The k-coefficients for close relatives can usually be determined by inspection. For more complex relationships, there are formulae relating the k-coefficients to the inbreeding coefficients (Crow and Kimura 1970, pp. 132–136). For close relatives and unrelated individuals, the values are given below, along with the numerical values for the example above. The likelihood ratio (LR) is the ratio of the match probability for the relatives divided by that for unrelated persons.

	k_2	$2k_1$	k_0	Joint prob.	LR
Full sibs	0.25	0.5	0.25	7.7×10^{-32}	10^6
Parent-child	0	1.00	0	0	0
Half-sibs	0	0.5	0.50	1.31×10^{-34}	2,000
Cousins	0	0.25	0.75	1.12×10^{-35}	170
Unrelated	0	0	1.00	6.47×10^{-38}	1

These two profiles are about a million times as likely if they came from sibs as if they were from unrelated persons. In fact, the two profiles actually were obtained from sibs. Note, from THO1, that a parent-child relation is ruled out, except for possible mutation. Note that the LR ratio for full sibs vs. half-sibs is $10^6/2,000$ or 500, so the profiles are much more likely if they are siblings than if they are half-siblings.

Siblings and other relatives offer one complication. Ordinarily, mutation does not matter, but in close relatives a mutation can alter the probabilities. This is not likely to be a problem, however, for two reasons: First, mutation is rare, even among STRs. Second, the effect of a mutation is to lower the likelihood ratio for relatives, so the bias is in favor of the defendant.

We have simplified the analysis in two ways: One is by neglecting the effects of population structure. The other is by assuming that neither the individuals nor their parents are inbred. This is usually sufficient for forensic analysis, but if a more realistic analysis is needed, general methods for all relatives, including inbred individuals, are given by Evett and Weir (1998), pp. 111–116.

References

Aitken, C. G. G. 1995. Statistics and the evaluation of evidence for forensic scientists. Wiley, New York.

Anderson, S., et al. 1981. Sequence and organization of the human mitochondrial genome. *Nature* 290: 457–465.

Awadalla, P., A. Eyre-Walker, and J. Maynard Smith. 1999. Linkage disequilibrium and recombination in hominid mitochondrial DNA. *Science* 286: 2524–2525.

Balding, D. J. 1997. Errors and misunderstandings in the second NRC Report. *Jurimetrics* 37: 603–607.

Balding, D. J. 1999. When can a DNA profile be regarded as unique? *Science and Justice* 39: 257–260.

Balding, D. J., and P. Donnelly. 1995. Inferring identity from DNA profile evidence. *Proc. Natl. Acad. Sci.* USA 92: 11741–11745.

Balding, D. J., and P. Donnelly. 1996. Evaluating DNA profile evidence when the suspect is identified through a database search. *J. Forensic Sci.* 41: 603–607.

Balding, D. J., and R. A. Nichols. 1994. DNA profile match probability calculations: How to allow for population stratification, relatedness, database selection and single bands. *Forensic Sci. Intern.* 64: 125–140.

Berg, P., and M. Singer. 1992. *Dealing with Genes: The Language of Heredity.* University Science Books, Mill Valley, CA.

Brenner, C. H. 1997. Probable race of a stain donor. Seventh International Symposium on Human Identification. pp. 48–52. Promega Inc., Madison, WI.

Brenner, C. H. 1998. Difficulties in the estimation of ethnic affiliation. *Amer. J. Hum. Genet.* 62: 1558–1560.

Brenner, S., S. R. Williams, E. H. Vermaas, et al. 2000. In vitro cloning of complex mixtures of DNA on microbeads: Physical separation of differentially expressed cDNAs. *Proc. Natl. Acad. Sci.* USA 97: 1665–1670.

Buckleton, John. 2000. Personal communication.

Budowle, B. 1995. The effects of inbreeding on DNA profile frequency estimates using PCR-based loci. *Genetica* 96: 21–25.

Budowle, B., J. A. Lindsey, J. A. DeCou, B. W. Koons, A. M. Giusti, and C. T. Comey. 1995. Validation and population studies of the loci LDLR, GYPA, HBGG, D7S8, and Gc (PM loci), and HLA-DQα using a multiplex amplification and typing procedure. *J. Forens. Sci.* 40: 45–54.

Budowle, B., R. Chakraborty, G. Carmody, and K. L. Monson. 2000. Source attribution of a forensic DNA profile. *Forens. Sci. Comm.* (in press).

Budowle, B., and R. R. Moretti. 1999. Genotype profiles for six population groups at the 13 CODIS short tandem repeat core loci and other PCR based loci. *Forensic Science Communications*, FBI Lab. Div. Pub. 99–06, U.S. Department of Justice.

Budowle, B., T. R. Moretti, A. L. Baumstark, D. A. Defenbaugh, and K. L. Keys. 1999. Population data on the thirteen CODIS core short tandem repeat loci in African-American, U.S. Caucasians, Hispanics, Bahamians, Jamaicans, and Trinidadians. *J. Forensic Sci.* 44: 1277–1286.

Budowle, B., B. Shea, S. Niezgoda, and R. Chakraborty. 2000. CODIS STR loci data from 41 sample populations. *J. Forens. Sci.* (in press).

Butler, J. M. 1998. The use of capillary electrophoresis in genotyping STR loci. *Methods Mol. Biol.* 98: 279–289.

Cavalli-Sforza, L. L., and W. F. Bodmer. 1971. *The Genetics of Human Populations.* W. H. Freeman, San Francisco, CA.

Cecil, J. S., and T. E. Willging. 1994. Court-appointed experts. Pp. 527–573 in *Reference Manual on Scientific Evidence.* Federal Judicial Center, Washington, DC.

Chakraborty, R. 1992. Sample size requirements for addressing the population genetics issues of forensic use of DNA typing. *Human Biol.* 64: 141–159.

Chakraborty, R. 2000. Personal communication.

Cockerham, C. C. 1967. Group inbreeding and coancestry. *Genetics* 56: 89–104.

Cockerham, C. C. 1969. Variance of gene frequencies. *Evolution* 23: 72–84.

Collins, A., and N. E. Morton. 1994. Likelihood ratios for DNA identification. *Proc. Natl. Acad. Sci.* USA. 91: 6007–6011.

Connors, E., T. Lundregan, N. Miller, and T. McEwen. 1996. *Convicted by Juries, Exonerated by Science: Case Studies in the Use of DNA Evidence to Establish Innocence After Trial.* U.S. Department of Justice, National Institute of Justice, Washington, DC.

Cotterman, C. W. 1940. A calculus for statistico-genetics. Reprinted as pp. 157–271 in Ballonoff, P. ed. *Genetics and Social Structure.* 1974. Dowden, Hutchinson, and Ross, Stroudsburg, PA.

Crow, J. F., and C. Denniston. 1993. Population genetics as it relates to human identification. pp. 31–35. Fourth International Symposium on Human Identification. Promega Inc., Madison, WI.

Crow, J. F., and M. Kimura. 1970. *An Introduction to Population Genetics Theory.* Harper and Row, New York. Reprinted by Burgess Publishing Company, Edina, MN.

Curran, J. M., C. M. Triggs, J. Buckleton, and B. S. Weir. 1999. Interpreting DNA mixtures in structured populations. *J. Forensic Sci.* 44: 987–995.

DAB. 2000. Statistical and population genetics issues affecting the evaluation of the frequency of occurrence of DNA profiles calculated from pertinent population databases. *Forens. Sci. Comm.* (in press).

Deka, R., M. D. Shriver, L. M. Yu, et al. 1999. Genetic variation at twenty-three microsatellite loci in sixteen human populations. *J. Genet.* 78: 99–121.

Donnelly, P., and R. E. Friedman. 1999. DNA database searches and the legal consumption of scientific evidence. *Michigan Law Rev.* 97: 931–984.

Erlich, H. A., ed. 1989. *PCR Technology. Principles and Applications for DNA Amplification.* Stockton, New York.

Evett, I. W. 1992. Evaluating DNA profiles in a case where the defense is 'It was my brother'. *J. Forensic Sci. Soc.* 32: 5–14.

Evett, I. W., and B. S. Weir. 1998. *Interpreting DNA Evidence.* Sinauer Associates, Sunderland, MA. Statistical and genetic methods.

Evett, I. W., R. Pinchin, and C. Buffery. 1992. An investigation of the feasibility of inferring ethnic origin from DNA profiles. *J. Forensic Sci. Soc.* 32: 301–306.

Eyre-Walker, A., N. H. Smith, and J. Maynard Smith. 1999. Mitochondrial DNA recombination-reasons to panic. *Proc. Roy. Soc.* B 266: 2037–2039.

FBI. 1993. *VNTR Population Data: A Worldwide Study.* Vols. I-A, I-B, II, III, IV. FBI Academy, Quantico, VA.

FBI. 1997. Press release. FBI Laboratory, Quantico, VA.

FBI. 1999. *1998 CODIS DNA Laboratory Survey.* FBI Forensic Science Systems Unit, FBI Laboratory, Quantico, VA.

Foreman, L. A., A. F. M. Smith, and I. W. Evett. 1999. Bayesian validation of a quadruplex STR profiling system for identification purposes. *J. Forensic Sci.* 44: 378–486.

Garofano, L., M. Pizzamiglio, V. Cesare, G. Lago, T. D'Errico, G. Brembilla, G.A. Romano, and B. Budowle. 1998. Italian population data on thirteen short tandem repeat loci. *Forens. Sci. Int.* 97: 53–60.

Greenfeld, L. A. 1997. *Sex offenses and offenders: an analysis of data on rape and sexual assault.* U.S. Department of Justice, Washington, DC.

Hammond, H. A., L. Jin., Y. Zhong, C. T. Caskey, and R. Chakraborty. 1994. Evaluation of 13 short tandem repeat loci for use in personal identification applications. *Amer. J. Hum. Genet.* 55: 175–189.

Hammond, H. and C. T. Caskey. 1997. *Automated DNA Typing: Method of the Future.* Research Preview. U.S. Department of Justice, National Institute of Justice, Washington, DC.

Hartl, D. L., and A. G. Clark. 1997. *Principles of Population Genetics*. 3rd Edition. Sinauer Associates, Sunderland, MA.

Hartmann, J. M., B. T. Houlihan, R. S. Keister, and E. L. Buse. 1997. The effect of ethnic and racial population substructuring on the estimation of multi-locus fixed-bin VNTR RFLP genotype probabilities. *J. Forensic Sci.* 42: 232–240.

Inman, K., and N. Rudin. 1997. *An Introduction to Forensic DNA Analysis*. CRC Press, Boca Raton, FL.

Inman, K., and N. Rudin. 2000. *Principles and Practice of Forensic Science*. CRC Press, Boca Raton, FL.

Innis, M. A., D. H. Gelfand, and J. J. Sninsky, eds. 1999. *PCR applications. Protocols for functional genomics*. Academic Press, New York.

Jeffreys, A. J., V. Wilson, and S. L. Thein. 1985a. Hypervariable minisatellite regions in human DNA. *Nature* 314: 67–72.

Jeffreys, A. J., V. Wilson, and S. L. Thein. 1985b. Individual specific "fingerprints" of human DNA. *Nature* 316: 75–79.

Kaye, D. H. 2000. Bioethics, bench, and bar: selected arguments in Landry v. Attorney General. *Jurimetrics* J. 40: 193–216.

Kaye, D. H., and G. F. Sensabaugh. 2000. Reference guide on forensic DNA evidence. In *Reference Manual on Scientific Evidence*. Federal Judicial Center, Washington, DC.

Kirby, L. T. 1992. *DNA Fingerprinting. An Introduction*. W. H. Freeman, New York.

Klitz, W., R. Reynolds, J. Chen, and H. A. Erlich. 2000. Analysis of genotype frequencies and interlocus association for the PM, DQA1, and D1S80 loci in four populations. *J. For. Sci.* (in press).

Krawczak, M., and J. Schmidtke. 1998. *DNA Fingerprinting*. 2nd Edition. BIOS. Scientific Publishers, Herndon, VA.

Landsteiner, K. 1900. Zur Kenntnis der antifermentativen, lytischen und agglutinierenden Wirkungen des Blutserums und der Lymphe. *Zent. Bact.* 27: 357–362.

Lewin, B. 1990. *Genes IV*. Oxford University Press, Oxford.

Lincoln, P. J, and J. Thompson. 1998. *Forensic DNA Profiling Protocols*. Humana Press, Totowa, NJ.

Lins, A. M., et al. 1998. Development and population study of an eight-locus short tandem repeat (STR) multiplex system. *J. Forens. Sci.* 43: 1–13.

Macaulay, V., M. Richards, and B. Sykes. 1999. Mitochondrial DNA recombination-no need to panic. *Proc. Roy. Soc.* B 266: 2037–2039.

Malakoff, D. 1999. Bayes offers a 'new' way to make sense of numbers. *Science* 286: 1460–1464.

Mange, E. J., and A. P. Mange. 1999. *Basic Human Genetics*. Sinauer Associates, Sunderland, MA.

Mayo, D. G. 1996. *Error and Growth of Experimental Knowledge*. University of Chicago Press, Chicago.

Morton, N. E. 1992. Genetic structure of forensic populations. *Proc. Natl. Acad. Sci. USA* 89: 2556–2560.

Morton, N. E. 1995. Alternative approaches to population structure. *Genetica* 96: 139–144.

Morton, N. E. 1997. The forensic DNA endgame. *Jurimetrics* 37: 477–494.

Mullis, K. B., F. Ferré, and R. A. Gibbs, ed. 1994. *The polymerase chain reaction*. Birkhauser, Boston, MA.

Mullis, K., and F. Faloona. 1987. Specific synthesis of DNA in vitro via a polymerase-catalyzed chain reaction. *Method. Enzymol.* 155: 335–350.

Nature Genetics. The chipping forecast. *Nat. Genet.* 21s: 1–60.

Nei, M. 1987. *Molecular Evolutionary Genetics*. Columbia University Press, New York.

NIJ. 1998. *Forensic Laboratories: Handbook for Facility Planning, Design, Construction, and Moving*. U.S. Department of Justice, National Institute of Justice, Washington, DC.

NIJ. 1999. *Eyewitness Evidence: A Guide for Law Enforcement*. U.S. Department of Justice, National Institute of Justice, Washington, DC.

NIJ. 2000. *Crime Scene Investigation: A Guide for Law Enforcement*. U.S. Department of Justice, National Institute of Justice, Washington, DC.

NRC. 1992. *DNA Technology in Forensic Science*. National Academy Press, Washington, DC.

NRC. 1996. *The Evaluation of Forensic DNA Evidence*. National Academy Press, Washington, DC.

Richie, K. L, M. D. Goldsborough, M. M. Darfler, E. A. Benzinger, M. L. Lovekemp, D. J. Reeder, and C. C. O'Connnell. 1999. Long PCR for VNTR analysis. *J. Forensic Sci.* 44: 1176–1185.

Righetti, P. G., and C. Gelfi. 1998. Recent advances in capillary zone electrophoresis of DNA. *Forensic Sci. Intern.* 92: 239–250.

Robertson, B., and G. A. Vigneaux. 1995. DNA evidence: wrong answers or wrong questions? *Genetica* 96: 145–152.

Robertson, B., and G. A. Vigneaux. 1992. Expert evidence: law, practice and probability. *Oxford J. Legal Studies* 12: 392–403.

Roeder, K. 1994. DNA fingerprinting: a review of the controversy. *Stat. Sci.* 9: 222–278.

Royall, R. 1997. *Statistical Evidence. A Likelihood Paradigm*. Chapman & Hall, New York.

Saiki, R., S. Scharf, F. Faloona, K. Mullis, G. Horn, H. A. Erlich, and N. Arnheim. 1985. Enzymatic amplification of β-globin genomic sequences and restriction site analysis for diagnosis of sickle cell anemia. *Science* 230: 1350–1354.

Saiki, R. K., D. H. Gelfand, S. Stoffel, S. Scharf, R. H. Higuchi, G. T. Horn, K. B. Mullis, and H. A. Erlich. 1988. Primer-directed enzymatic amplification of DNA with a thermostable DNA polymerase. *Science* 239: 487–491.

Schmalzing, D., A. Adourian, L. Koutny, L, Ziaugra, P. Matsudaira, and D. Ehrlich. 1998. DNA sequencing on microfabricated electrophoretic devices. *Analytical Chem.* 70: 2303–2310.

Schmalzing, D., L. Koutny, D. Chisholm, A. Adourian, P. Matsudaira, and D. Ehrlich. 1999. Two-color multiplexed analysis of eight short tandem repeat loci with an electro-phoretic microdevice. *Anal. Biochem.* 270: 148–152.

Schumm, J. 1999. Personal communication.

Sensabaugh, G., and D. H. Kaye. 1998. Non-human DNA evidence. *Jurimetrics* 38: 1–16.

Shriver, M. D., M. W. Smith, L. Jin, A. Marcini, J. M. Akey, R. Deka, and R. E. Ferrell. 1997. Ethnic-affiliation estimation by use of population-specific DNA markers. *Amer. J. Hum. Genet.* 60: 957–964.

Siebert, P. 1998. *The PCR technique: RT-PCR*. Eaton Pub. Co. The technique for amplifying DNA from RNA sources.

Snustad, D. P., and M. J. Simmons. 2000. *Principles of Genetics*. 2nd Edition. John Wiley, New York.

Stockmarr, A. 1999. Likelihood ratios for evaluating DNA evidence when the suspect is found through a database search. *Biometrics* 55: 671–677.

Thormann, W., A. B. Wey, I. S. Lurie, H. Gerber, C. Byland, N. Malik, M. Hochmeister, and C. Gehrig. 1999. Capillary electrophoresis in clinical and forensic analysis: recent advances and breakthrough to routine applications. *Electrophoresis* 20: 3203–3236.

Tietz, D., ed. 1998. *Nucleic Acid Electrophoresis*. Springer-Verlag, New York.

Twyman, P. M. 1998. *Advanced Molecular Biology. A Concise Reference*. Springer-Verlag, New York.

Vieland, V. J., and S. E. Hodge. 1999. Review: Royal, Statistical Evidence. *Amer. J. Hum. Genet.* 63: 283–289.

Walker, R. H., Ed. 1983. *Inclusion Probabilities in Parentage Testing*. American Association of Blood Banks, Arlington, VA.

Watson, J. D., et al. 1987. *The Molecular Biology of the Gene*. Vols I and II. Benjamin/Cummings, Menlo Park, CA.

Weedn, V., and J. W. Hicks. 1998. *The Unrealized Potential of DNA Testing*. U.S. Department of Justice, National Institute of Justice, Washington, DC.

Weir, B. S., ed. 1995. Human identification: the use of DNA markers. *Genetica* 96: 1–178.

Weir, B. S. 1994. Effects of inbreeding on forensic calculations. *Ann. Rev. Genet.* 28: 597–621.

Weir, B. S., ed. 1995. *Human Identification*. Kluwer, Amsterdam.

Weir, B. S. 1996. *Genetic Data Analysis II*. Sinauer, Sunderland, MA.

Weir, B. S. 1999. Are DNA profiles unique? Proceedings of the Ninth International Symposium on Human Identification. pp. 114–117. Promega Corp., Madison, WI.

Weir, B. S., C. M. Triggs, L, I. Starling, K. A. J. Walsh, and J. Buckleton. 1997. Interpreting DNA mixtures. *J. Forensic Sci.* 42: 213–222.

Word, C. J., T. M. Sawosick, and D. H. Bing. 1997. Summary of validation studies from twenty-six forensic laboratories in the United States and Canada on the use of the AmpliType PM PCR amplification and typing kit. *J. For. Sci.* 42: 39–48.

Wright, S. 1951. The genetical structure of populations. *Ann. Eugen.* 15: 159–171.

Wyman, A. R., and R. White. 1980. A highly polymorphic locus in human DNA. *Proc. Natl. Acad. Sci.* USA 77: 6754–6758.

Xiong, M., and L. Jin. 1999. Comparison of the power and accuracy of biallelic and microsatellite markers in population-based gene-mapping methods. *Amer. J. Hum. Genet.* 64: 629–640.

Abbreviations and Acronyms

ABC	American Board of Criminalistics
AFIP	Armed Forces Institute of Pathology
ASCLD	American Society of Crime Laboratory Directors
ATB	Advanced Technology Board
ATP	Advanced Technology Program (NIST)
CAP	College of American Pathologists
CE	Capillary electrophoresis
CODIS	Combined DNA Index System
DAB	DNA Advisory Board
EST	Expressed sequence tag
FSS	Forensic Science Service
HV1, HV2	Hypervariable regions in mitochondrial DNA
HW	Hardy-Weinberg
LE	Linkage equilibrium
mtDNA	Mitochondrial DNA
mu(μ)	Micrometer; one millionth of a meter
NCIC	National Crime Index Computer
NCJRS	National Criminal Justice Reference Service
NDIS	National DNA Index System
ng	Nanogram; one billionth of a gram
NIJ	National Institute of Justice
NIST	National Institute of Standards and Technology
OLES	Office of Law Enforcement Standards
PCR	Polymerase chain reaction
PM	Polymarker
RFLP	Restriction fragment length polymorphism
SNP	Single nucleotide polymorphism
SSO	Sequence specific oligonucleotids
STR	Short tandem repeats
SWGDAM	Scientific Working Group on DNA Analysis Methods
TWGDAM	Technical Working Group on DNA Analysis Methods
TWGNAS	Technical Working Group on Nucleic Acid Standards
VNTR	Variable number of tandem repeats

Glossary

(Note: Many of these definitions are taken from NRC 1996, which may be consulted for a more extensive list.)

Adenine: One of the four bases in DNA; abbreviated A.

Allele: One of two or more alternative forms of a gene. In DNA identification, the definition is extended to any DNA region used for analysis.

Amelogenin: A system that generates different sized fragments for the X and Y chromosomes, and hence is used for sex identification.

Amplification: Producing multiple copies of a chosen DNA region, usually by PCR.

Autosome: Any chromosome other than the X and Y.

Binning: Grouping VNTR alleles into sets of similar sizes, necessary because the individual alleles are too similar to differentiate.

Chip: A miniaturized system for DNA analysis. It uses photolithography and chemical etching of a silicon or glass wafer to produce microchannels that transport sample DNA, the movement of which is detected by a laser beam.

Chromosome: A physical structure in the cell nucleus. It consists of a tightly coiled thread of DNA with associated proteins and RNA. The genes are arranged in linear order along the DNA.

Confidence interval, confidence limits: An interval, based on a sample, that is expected to include the population mean value a specified proportion of the time (e.g., 95 percent).

Crossing over: The exchange of parts between homologous chromosomes during meiosis; recombination.

Cytosine: One of the four bases in DNA; abbreviated C.

Denaturation: Separation of double stranded DNA into single strands.

Deoxyribonucleic acid (DNA): The genetic material; a double helix composed of two complementary chains of paired bases (nucleotides).

Electrophoresis: A technique in which different molecules are separated by their rate of movement, usually through a gel, in an electric field.

Expressed sequence tag: A fragment of DNA associated with a particular gene that can be used for gene identification.

Gamete: A haploid reproductive cell; sperm or egg.

Gene: The basic unit of heredity; a functional sequence of DNA in a chromosome.

Genome: The total (haploid) genetic makeup of an organism. In the human this comprises about 3 billion base pairs.

Genotype: The genetic makeup of an individual, as distinguished from its manifestation (phenotype); usually designated by allele symbols, e.g., A_1A_2 designates the genotype of an individual with alleles A_1 and A_2. The word is used to designate any number of loci.

Guanine: One of the four bases in DNA; abbreviated G.

Haploid: Having one set of chromosomes, as a gamete (cf. *diploid*).

Hardy-Weinberg proportions: The state, for a genetic locus in a population, in which the alleles making up the genotype are in random proportions.

Heterozygosity: The proportion of a population that is heterozygous for a particular locus.

Heterozygote: A fertilized egg (*zygote*) with two different alleles at a designated locus; by extension, the individual that develops from such a zygote (cf. *homozygote*).

Homologous: Corresponding; used to describe the relationship between two members of a chromosome or gene pair.

Homozygote: A fertilized egg (*zygote*) with two identical alleles at a designated locus; by extension, the individual that develops from such a zygote (cf. *heterozygote*).

Inbreeding coefficient: The probability that two alleles in an individual are descended from the same allele in a common ancestor, or one from the other; a measure of the proportion by which the heterozygosity is reduced by inbreeding; designated by F_i.

Kinship coefficient: The probability that two randomly chosen alleles, one from each of two individuals in a population, are identical (i.e., both descended from the same ancestral allele, or one from the other); equivalent to the inbreeding coefficient of a (perhaps hypothetical) offspring; designated by F_{ij}.

Linkage: Inheritance together of two or more genes on the same chromosome.

Linkage equilibrium: The state in which two or more loci in a gamete are in random proportions (i.e., the gamete frequency is the product of the allele frequencies); abbreviated LE.

Locus (pl. loci): The physical location of a gene (or DNA region of interest) on a chromosome.

Marker: An easily detected gene or chromosome region used for identification.

Meiosis: The two cell divisions that occur in the development of a sperm or egg, during which the chromosome number is halved.

Micron: One millionth of a meter (abbreviated μ)

Mitochondrial DNA: DNA in the mitochondria.

Mitochondrion (pl. mitochondria): A particle present in multiple copies per cell and transmitted from the mother to all her children.

Mitosis: The process of cell division in which the chromosomes are precisely distributed so that the parent and each daughter cell have the same chromosome content.

Multiplex: A system for analyzing several loci at once.

Nucleotide: A unit of DNA composed of phosphate, a sugar and a purine or pyrimidine base.

Phenotype: The recognizable manifestation of the genotype; it may be externally visible, as hair color, or observed by a special technique, as blood groups or enzymes.

Polymerase chain reaction: An in vitro process for making many copies of a chosen fragment of DNA; abbreviated PCR.

Polymorphism: The presence of more than one allele at a locus in a population; usually the word is used only when at least two alleles are fairly common.

Quality assurance: A program conducted by a laboratory to ensure accuracy and reliability of tests performed.

Quality control: Activities used to monitor the quality of DNA typing to satisfy specified criteria.

Random match: A match in the DNA profiles of two DNA samples, where one is drawn at random from the population.

Random-match probability: The probability that the DNA in a random sample from the population has the same profile as the DNA in the evidence sample.

Restriction enzyme, restriction endonuclease: An enzyme that cuts a DNA molecule in a specified short base sequence.

Restriction fragment length polymorphism: Variation in the length of a stretch of DNA; abbreviated RFLP.

Ribonucleic acid: The product of transcription from DNA; abbreviated RNA.

Sex chromosomes: The X and Y chromosomes.

Short tandem repeat: A tandem repeats in which the repeat units are three, four, or five base pairs; abbreviated STR.

Single nucleotide probe: A probe that detects a single base change at a specific location.

Somatic cells: Body cells; cells other than those in the cellular ancestry of egg and sperm.

Southern blotting: The technique for transferring DNA fragments that have been separated by electrophoresis from the gel to a membrane (usually nylon).

Thymine: One of the four bases in DNA; abbreviated T.

Uracil: A base in RNA, corresponding to T in DNA; abbreviated U.

Variable number of tandem repeats: Repeating units of a DNA sequence; a class of RFLPs; abbreviated VNTR.

X chromosome: A sex chromosome, present twice in female cells and once in male.

Y chromosome: A sex chromosome present once in males, and transmitted directly from a father to all his sons.

Zygote: A diploid cell produced by fusion of an egg and sperm.

About the National Institute of Justice

The National Institute of Justice (NIJ), a component of the Office of Justice Programs, is the research agency of the U.S. Department of Justice. Created by the Omnibus Crime Control and Safe Streets Act of 1968, as amended, NIJ is authorized to support research, evaluation, and demonstration programs; development of technology; and both national and international information dissemination. Specific mandates of the Act direct NIJ to:

- Sponsor special projects and research and development programs that will improve and strengthen the criminal justice system and reduce or prevent crime.

- Conduct national demonstration projects that employ innovative or promising approaches for improving criminal justice.

- Develop new technologies to fight crime and improve criminal justice.

- Evaluate the effectiveness of criminal justice programs and identify programs that promise to be successful if continued or repeated.

- Recommend actions that can be taken by Federal, State, and local governments as well as by private organizations to improve criminal justice.

- Carry out research on criminal behavior.

- Develop new methods of crime prevention and reduction of crime and delinquency.

In recent years, NIJ has greatly expanded its initiatives, the result of the Violent Crime Control and Law Enforcement Act of 1994 (the Crime Act), partnerships with other Federal agencies and private foundations, advances in technology, and a new international focus. Examples of these new initiatives include:

- Exploring key issues in community policing, violence against women, violence within the family, sentencing reforms, and specialized courts such as drug courts.

- Developing dual-use technologies to support national defense and local law enforcement needs.

- Establishing four regional National Law Enforcement and Corrections Technology Centers and a Border Research and Technology Center.

- Strengthening NIJ's links with the international community through participation in the United Nations network of criminological institutes, the U.N. Criminal Justice Information Network, and the NIJ International Center.

- Improving the online capability of NIJ's criminal justice information clearinghouse.

- Establishing the ADAM (Arrestee Drug Abuse Monitoring) program—formerly the Drug Use Forecasting (DUF) program—to increase the number of drug-testing sites and study drug-related crime.

The Institute Director establishes the Institute's objectives, guided by the priorities of the Office of Justice Programs, the Department of Justice, and the needs of the criminal justice field. The Institute actively solicits the views of criminal justice professionals and researchers in the continuing search for answers that inform public policymaking in crime and justice.

To find out more about the National Institute of Justice,
please contact:

National Criminal Justice Reference Service
P.O. Box 6000
Rockville, MD 20849–6000
800–851–3420
e-mail: *askncjrs@ncjrs.org*

To obtain an electronic version of this document, access the NIJ Web site
(*http://www.ojp.usdoj.gov/nij*).

If you have questions, call or e-mail NCJRS.

www.ingramcontent.com/pod-product-compliance
Lightning Source LLC
Chambersburg PA
CBHW081549170526

45166CB00009B/2636